RUSSIAN GYPSY TALES

3-93

collected by
Yefim Druts & Alexei Gessler

translated by
James Riordan

INTERLINK
NEW YO

D1202993

First American edition published 1992 by

INTERLINK BOOKS
An imprint of Interlink Publishing Group, Inc.
99 Seventh Avenue
Brooklyn, New York 11215

Originally published by Canongate Press Ltd., Edinburgh

Library of Congress Cataloging-in-Publication Data

Russian gypsy tales / collected by Yefim Druts & Alexei Gessler ;
translated by James Riordan.
    p. cm.
    ISBN 1–56656–100–0 — ISBN 0–940793–97–0 (pbk.)
    1. Gypsies—Russian S.F.S.R.—Folklore. 2. Tales—Russian
S.F.S.R. I. Druts, E. (Efim), 1937– . II. Gessler, A.
(Aleksei), 1945– . III. Riordan, James, 1936–
GR203.17.R86   1992
398.2′08991497047—dc20   92–7316
                                              CIP

Printed and bound in the United States of America
10 9 8 7 6 5 4 3 2 1

But there is no happiness even amongst you,
Poor sons of nature . . .
And beneath your tattered tents
Live tormenting dreams,
And your nomadic abodes
In the wilderness have not escaped misfortune,
Fateful passions are everywhere,
And there is no escaping fate.

Alexander Pushkin: *Tsygany* (The Gypsies)

CONTENTS

CONTENTS

INTRODUCTION

Many centuries have passed since the dusky, dark-haired people left their home to wander the five continents of the world. Today they are to be found as far apart as the Yorkshire moors and the Siberian steppe, the Mexican sierra and the Sahara desert, and the city squares of Washington and Sydney. Home has long ceased to be home.

When Europeans first met them, some wanderers proudly said they were descendants of the Egyptian Pharaohs. So the British called them *Gypsies* (from the word Egypt); the Spanish called them *Gitanos*, while Hungarians used the term "Pharaoh's People." Others named them from the Greek *atsingan*, a sect famed for its fortune-telling; hence the German *Zigeuner* and the Russian *tsygan*. They called themselves *Rom* or *Romaly*—the People.

It was only when their language and folklore were studied properly in the nineteenth century that the mystery of their origin was resolved. Scholars found their language to be close to the ancient Indian tongue of Sanskrit and to modern Hindi; their origins were traced to northern India, the Punjab, which at one time had formed the cradle of the Rom nation. They had evidently fled in the tenth and eleventh centuries to escape warring neighbors and their "untouchable" caste status in society. So began the long, hard, dangerous trek of Rom tribes about the world.

In the lands they entered, local people regarded them at best with suspicion, more often with hostility. After all, they

were intruders, outcasts, who camped in pastures and meadows, paid no taxes, helped themselves to grain from fields, and sometimes robbed to survive. Wherever they pitched their tents or hitched the horses of their caravans they tried to make a living: following their old Indian profession as dancers and entertainers, telling fortunes, horse-dealing, or horse-curing.

Almost everywhere they were bullied and driven on, banned from certain trades and cities, sometimes hanged, and burned at the stake. And not only in our barbaric past. In our "civilized" present over 30,000 Rom men, women and children were put to death by the Nazis during the Second World War. Even today, almost everywhere, Roms are denied open space, respect, even the right to settle. The old Rom plea still stands,

> I don't beg for bread
> Even though I'm hungry.
> Just give the Rom
> A little respect.

Roms come to Russia

They came to Russia at different times by various routes. The "southerners" wandered up through the Balkans to camp around the Black Sea and the Ukraine in the fourteenth century; the "northerners" arrived in the north of Russia a century or two later via Germany and Poland. In such a vast expanse as Russia it was not hard to find shelter and safety in forest and steppe ("the forest is safer than the market place" as the old Rom saying has it); and they mingled with other colorful nationalities of the sprawling Russian empire—Tartars and Eskimos, Georgians and Armenians, Moldavians, Ukrainians and Russians. They wandered in large clans in the sunny, fertile south, but in smaller tribes in the harsh, cold north.

Then, as now, the authorities tried to persuade, tax and cajole them into settled farming, to impose Russian laws, faith and customs upon them. Even as recently as 1956 they were banned from traveling on the road, from living as nomads; but that has not stopped them entirely, as any Russian will testify.

True, some Roms have now settled in their own horse-breeding co-operative farms; some tour the country in song and dance groups; some perform in the world's only Rom theater—the *Romany* in Moscow; some have become doctors, engineers, writers and scholars, as elsewhere. And some still roam and tell fortunes, as of old. Of the world's estimated six million Roms, some 210,000 today live in what used to be the Soviet Union.

As for Rom folklore, it is a rich brew of native and borrowed cultures and ancient traditions. In their music, for example, they have long learned to earn a living by taking up the national instruments of other peoples: the violin and guitar, tambourine and drum. True Rom songs and dances possess no accompaniment save hand-clapping, as in the Rom (flamenco) dances of Spain. In folk tales too, as in their faith, they took the external forms of customs and beliefs of their adopted land; they have no body of historical legends, no national heroes of their own.

What Rom tales do contain is a lingering custom handed down from times gone by, the dimly recalled story of exile and persecution, of their homelands and wanderings abroad, of scraping a living, and the often unsconscious adaptation of the folk tales of other peoples to their story-telling.

The tales in this collection lift just a corner of the curtain that obscures Russian Rom traditions, mysteries, and beliefs. We sense the importance of the family, the tribe and the clan. We see the chieftain, *vaida*, whose word is law, who decides the time and direction of wandering, the mode of survival. It is

he (it is always *he*) or the council of elders (always male) who settle disputes, as when a member breaks a promise or fails to repay a debt—cases of stealing from or killing other Roms are extremely rare. It is the chieftain who decides who marries whom. He also decides when a dying tribe member is to be taken outside the tent or caravan and left alone to perish. Very few Roms would go against the chieftain, the tribe, or break a tribal vow, not so much from superstition as from fear of being driven out of the camp in shame. No one would have dealings with a shamed person or any member of that person's family. It was much strong discipline and loyalty that helped bind a tribe together.

The folk tales describe a male-ordered society. Women not only looked after home and family, they were often responsible for earning the living as well. Traditionally, men were privileged, their work confined to horses and crafts. They would buy and sell horses, ride expertly, diagnose all horse ailments and prescribe cures. In Russia they had a reputation as fine craftsmen: as jewelry-fashioners, makers of pots and pans, basket-weavers, wood-carvers and smiths. There are many legends that tell, for example, of Roms who are descendants of the smiths who made the nails for the Crucifixion; or of Roms who stole the fourth nail from the cross; or of the Rom hanged alongside Christ. That is why Roms were doomed to roam the earth for seven years or seven centuries.

The obvious difference shown by Rom women in appearance, clothing, language and skilful talk certainly encouraged their popularity as fortune-tellers. The folk tales demonstrate, however, that they themselves put much more trust in their own experience of life than in lines on a hand, voices from a finger tapping on an upturned glass, tea leaves in a cup, or the fall of the cards.

Russian Rom tales refer to God as *Deval*, and Satan as *Bengel* or *Beng* who appears in many tales as the evil genius or hero; it may be that Russian Roms saw themselves more as the persecuted devil than the god of their oppressors. In any case, as the Rom saying has it, "God is to be found in the forest, not in the church."

Here, then, is a glimpse into the life and beliefs of the Russian Rom. May the reading of the tales bring you luck, put the wind forever at your back, and find you a place in heaven long before the devil finds you gone.

James Riordan

VAIDA AND RUZHA

There were once some gypsies living on the estate of a friendly prince; they were rich and owned many fine steeds, none better than the champion racer Samuil. And the gypsies had a son, Vaida, who grew up into a proud and handsome young man.

One day, the lad went to his father and asked, "Father, why do I live alone like a holy candle? Is it not time for me to wed? Bless me, Father, and I will go in search of a bride."

"God will bless you," his father replied, "and we give our blessing too. Whom do you intend to wed?"

"I do not know yet. Tell me where wealthy gypsies live and I will go among them to seek my bride."

"There are some gypsies," his father said. "They live far from here, beyond the Dnepr River. And they have a beautiful daughter, Ruzha. But it won't be easy: many princes and merchants, gypsies and *gadjes* have tried to woo her – but she refused them all. And remember this: beware of her brothers!"

"Very well, Father," Vaida said. "We are born once into this world and leave it once. I shall be careful."

Vaida dressed in his richest attire, saddled the steed Samuil and rode off to seek his bride. God alone knows how long he was on his way, but eventually he came to the Dnepr River, dismounted, stood before the waves and said to Samuil, "What shall we do now?"

The horse understood the gypsy tongue. He neighed and

1

pawed the ground, then tossed his head, as if pointing to the other side. Vaida smiled and jumped into the saddle, shouting, "Ai-yai, Samuil, we die only once!"

They entered the water and swam across.

On the other side stood a rich gypsy camp; it was here that Ruzha lived. As he rode into the camp, Ruzha's brothers came forward to meet him, asking, "Who are you, where are you from?"

"Hey, Romaly, Romaly, all these questions before I've drunk some tea! See how wet I am. Hand me a bowl of tea and then we shall speak."

Vaida dried off by the fire while the gypsies unsaddled Samuil and set him to graze in the wild grass. And they and Vaida began their talk. In the midst of their conversation Vaida noticed Ruzha leave her tent; and as he gazed after her, his eyes grew misty, his dark hair stood on end. Never had he seen such beauty in all his life.

And when Ruzha caught sight of the handsome stranger she too fell in love at once, thinking to herself, "There sits my destiny."

But her father's shout rudely interrupted her thoughts.

"Put the kettle on, girl, we'll treat the young lord."

They brewed tea, drank and dined. And as they sat round the fire drinking tea, Vaida and Ruzha exchanged glances. And when an opportunity came, Vaida whispered into the young maid's ear, "After the meal take me aside as if you wish to tell my fortune."

And so she did. Hardly had they finished their eating than she rose, calling brightly, "Young man, I wish to tell your fortune."

"Tell away, dear lady," he said with a smile, "I've heard they tell good fortunes here. That's why I've come. I had a great misfortune and wish to know what I should do."

You should know, good folk, that Vaida did not want to

2

reveal he was a gypsy, lest he alert Ruzha's brothers – they might guess his intentions as suitor. So he spoke not a word in the gypsy tongue.

Ruzha led him to her tent, but not before a brother whispered, "Dear sister Ruzha, see if you can take the *gadje*'s rich waistcoat off him."

So before she began to tell his fortune, Ruzha made her request to appease her brother, "Sir, will you not give your fine waistcoat to my brother? He has set his heart on it."

Straightaway Vaida took off his waistcoat, saying, "Give it to him, with my compliments."

As Ruzha started to tell his fortune, Vaida suddenly interrupted her, "Do your brothers have racing horses?"

"Our horses have no rivals," she replied, "neither among rich nor poor, gypsies nor *gadjes*."

"Tell your brothers, dear Ruzha, I wish to race against them. And this is what I'll do: after two circuits I'll grab you by the hair and pull you into the saddle – and we'll be away. Don't worry, I have faith in my mount Samuil. First tell your father I want to trade horses."

So Ruzha went to her father and the old man at once hurried to take a look at Samuil.

"I'm an old gypsy, I know a thing or two about horses," he muttered to Vaida, first examining the horse's teeth. "Well now, *chiavala*, not a bad horse at all."

He prodded and tugged: mane, fetlocks, withers, croup . . .

"*Why not?* Let's talk business."

"Very well," said Vaida. "Only let's start this way. Saddle up your best horse to race against mine. We'll do two circuits of the clearing and see which wins."

Agreed. The horses were saddled and the first circuit was run. At first Samuil lagged behind, then drew level and, on the second run, left the other horse way behind. Without a pause Vaida rode over to Ruzha, seized her by her long black hair,

3

slung her across the saddle and raced away like the wind.

"Ai-yai-yai!" shouted the gypsies.

But Vaida was already on the other side of the Dnepr.

When Vaida and Ruzha reached Vaida's home they were swiftly wed, and then set out to take the news to the bride's family. That had to be done. After all, no one wants bad blood between two clans.

The deed being done, old quarrels were set aside and a great wedding feast was held.

After several days of feasting the happy pair returned once more to live with Vaida's parents. One year passed, and then another, and in the course of time Ruzha was with child. How pleased Vaida was. He did everything for his dear wife, carrying her everywhere in his arms, doing all she asked, all the cooking and housework.

His mother was most displeased.

"A man should not do women's work," she muttered, and hatred for Ruzha began to poison her mind.

One day, Ruzha asked Vaida to bring her some fish.

And off he rode to a distant lake. How long he was gone I cannot say, but Vaida's mother had overheard her request. And it made her more furious than ever.

Down to the stream she went, caught a poisonous snake, cooked it and gave Ruzha some to taste. The moment the poor girl tasted a piece she fell ill: her stomach ached, a fever coursed through her veins.

"That fish has made me poorly, Mama," she complained.

"Just lie down, my dear, you'll feel better soon."

"No, Mama, I want to go to meet my husband," groaned the sick girl.

As Ruzha went out to meet Vaida, she passed through the garden gate and suddenly halted, clutching her side. And slowly her lovely form turned into a rowan tree!

And there she stood, with red berries and green leaves.

5

"Where is my dear wife?" asked Vaida when he came home.

"But she went to meet you," his mother said.

As he retraced his steps and passed through the gate, he suddenly stopped and stared: what was this? He had passed by the fence many times, yet never had he seen a rowan tree growing there!

"I must take some rowan blossom to my wife," he sighed.

But the rowan answered him in a human voice, "Dear Vaida, don't break my bones."

With a start he stretched out his hands to touch the rowan tree, yet as he did so he turned into a spreading oak standing beside the rowan.

Thereupon his faithful mount Samuil began to neigh – and at once turned into a clump of heather; meanwhile the saddle which had fallen off turned into a snowball bush.

Some time later Vaida's father, tired of waiting for his son and daughter, went outside to investigate. And as he passed through the gate he stopped in surprise.

"I must be getting old," he said, scratching his head. "Nothing ever grew here surely, but look now: an oak and rowan, heather and a snowball bush!"

He stared and stared, then gradually the truth began to dawn. He knew of his wife's skill at sorcery and her hatred for their son's wife.

Reluctantly he summoned the gypsy court, and they called Vaida's mother to answer for her sins. At first she would not confess, but once she had taken the gypsy oath she had to tell the truth: how she had caught the snake, fed it to Ruzha and all that had followed.

She had to be punished the gypsy way; she was tied to a horse's tail and set flying across the open plain. So badly crushed was she by the flying hoofs that nothing was left of the wicked woman.

But I'll tell you this: to this day, wherever gypsies roam, they will call the rowan Ruzha, the oak Vaida, the heather the good steed Samuil, and the snowball bush the gypsy saddle.

THE ENCHANTED HINNY*

There was once a wealthy gypsy. He dealt in horses and earned himself a fortune. However, as the days passed over, his good wife died and left him a little son. How was he to bring up the boy?

There was nothing for it but to take another wife. This he did, though misfortune followed. How he grieved for his first wife and poured all his love upon the son who so resembled his dead mother! Well, as you may guess, the stepmother did not take to this at all, disliked her stepson, and was ever complaining to her mother, "What d'you think? The moment he returns from market he runs to that brat of his, and gives me no love at all."

And the two women stoked the fires of jealousy.

One time the gypsy made ready for a horse fair and asked his beloved son, "What gift shall I bring you?"

"Nothing special, father," his son replied. "But if it pleases you, fetch me the first thing you set eyes on as you enter town."

The gypsy harnessed his horses and galloped off. On entering town he looked about and spied an old fellow on a horse, and tied to the horse's tail was a pint-sized hinny. Recalling his son's words, he approached the rider, saying, "Hey there, *mora*, what price that hinny?"

"One ruble and a half, and God bless you."

*Hinny: offspring of a stallion and a donkey.

8

The gypsy grumbled at the price, but handed over the coins and went about his business at the fair. On returning home, he called to his son, "Your present's here: I bought it on the very edge of town."

When the boy saw his gift he was overjoyed; he petted and fretted over the hinny, gave it food and drink, and would not be parted from it. Thus it continued from then on.

As the gypsy boy grew older he became strong and handsome; and the handsomer he grew the less his stepmother liked him. Once when the father was not home, she went to her mother for advice: "How can I rid myself of that pest?"

The old dame took some poison, mixed it with dough, baked some rolls and told her daughter, "Give him these rolls: one bite will dispatch him to the other world."

So the stepmother returned home, made the rolls and told her stepson, "Here are some rolls, milk and cheese, go to the woods and gather firewood."

Just as the gypsy lad was leaving, he heard his hinny neighing from the stable. And as he went to investigate he heard a human voice: "Eat the milk and cheese, but give the dogs your rolls."

He did as the hinny said and was amazed to see the dogs roll over dead the moment they touched the poisoned rolls. From then on he loved the hinny even more. It had clearly saved his life.

When she saw the dead dogs lying in the yard, the stepmother hurried to her mother for advice.

"This and that, one thing and another, dead dogs and so on . . ."

So the mother said, "It can only be a spirit watching over him; we must outwit it somehow." And she handed her daughter a shirt, saying, "This is no ordinary shirt; when he puts it on he'll burn to a cinder."

As soon as the stepmother came home, she called her stepson to her. "I've heated some water; take a wash and put on this clean new shirt."

Just as the lad was about to wash he heard the hinny neigh from the stable. And when he ran to it, the hinny warned him in a human voice, "Don't put on that new shirt; throw it in the oven."

That he did. But the moment he cast the new shirt into the oven, flames flared up, black and orange, and the oven burst asunder with the heat. A third time the stepmother ran to her aged mother, complaining, "Nothing seems to harm that gypsy."

"Wait, my dear," her mother said. "I'll find out what spirit protects him."

Thereupon she lit a fire and gazed into the flickering flames. "Aha, I see the meddler now. Take that hinny from the stable, and all will be well!"

The stepmother arrived home just as her husband was returning.

"My darling husband," she murmured sweetly, stroking his cheek, "if you love me do me a favor: get rid of that hinny. It gives me no peace with all its neighing, and bites me each time I come near."

What was he to do? He loved his son and feared his wife. At last he told the boy, "We'll have to drive the hinny from our yard."

In deep despair, the lad went to give his pet the news.

"Don't fret," the hinny said. "Tell your father this: you wish to ride me one last time. Once you are on my back, we'll fly beyond the lofty mountains and seek our fortune elsewhere."

As it was said, so it was read. The father allowed the boy to take a final ride upon the hinny; yet no sooner had he sat upon its back than the hinny flew up higher than the lofty mountains and disappeared from view.

Together the gypsy and his hinny saw many sights upon their way, and came at last to a distant realm. As they landed beside the city walls, the hinny told the lad, "Listen well: catch a sheep and skin it, then cover your head with its fleece so that no one will recognize you. And should folk ask who you are and whence you come, tell them you know not how."

A sheep was caught and skinned, and as they entered the town a watchman stopped them at the gates, much astounded at the sight: an ass not an ass followed by a man not a man, a beast not a beast, sheep's head on human body. The Czar had to be informed.

Summoned forthwith to the Czar, to all questions he replied he knew not how. At last the Czar appointed him to the kitchens.

So Know Not How was set to work in the royal kitchens, while his hinny was stabled in the palace yard. One day the royal chef sent the new cook for firewood. Equipped with ax and rope, he set off for the forest and quickly came upon an oak standing tall and strong – wide enough to take a gypsy camp beneath its branches. Without more ado, he cut down the oak and hacked it into handy logs. When the job was done he tied them up in bundles and dragged them back to the palace, much to the amazement of the cooks.

"Where did you find so much wood?" they cried.

He told them of the oak: in such-and-such a place over by you-know-what tree.

That set them howling in distress.

"You've chopped down the Czar's favorite oak!"

Off dashed the cooks to inform the Czar, who realized, wise man, that Know Not How was no simpleton, but a man of superhuman strength.

You ought to know, dear folk, that upon that realm there lay an awful curse. Three sea monsters dwelt in the ocean surrounding the land and they, evil creatures, were demanding

11

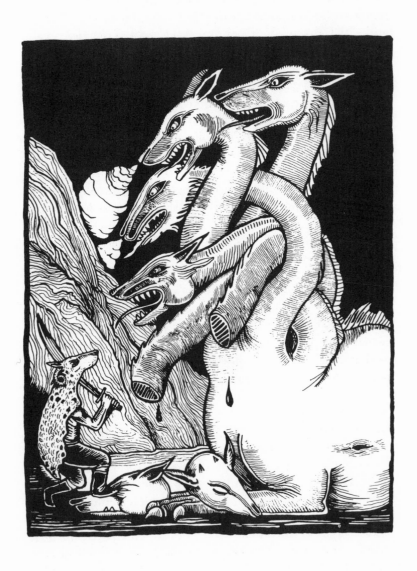

the royal princesses for their brides. It was now time for the first princess to go to her fate.

Meanwhile the poor Czar had sent riders to the ends of the earth to seek a man who could save his girls from their dreadful fate. And three brave men from overseas took up the challenge. Our gypsy, having had instruction from the enchanted hinny, was also ready for the fray.

Early one morning the eldest princess was led down to the sea, set inside a tower and abandoned to her fate. Meanwhile, the three brave men lay hidden behind the tower – awaiting the sea monster's appearance from the depths. All of a sudden, the sea seethed and foamed, and a six-headed monster crawled on to the shore: smoke billowed from his nostrils, the ground shook as he moved along and – Oh dear me! – the moment the three saviors saw that, they turned and fled, leaving the poor princess to her fate.

But then, from out of nowhere, the hinny landed with the sheep's-head gypsy on its back. How the monster roared with laughter at the sight of this sheep's-head lad.

"Thanks be to the Czar for his gracious gift," he roared. "Here comes my wedding supper too."

"I'm not here to sharpen your teeth," cried the lad. "I'm here to stop you tormenting the fair princess."

Thereupon he swung his sword and struck off three of the monster's heads. But the beast reared up and forced the gypsy into the damp soft sand; with his free hand, however, he could still wield his sword and sent the last three heads rolling down the strand.

The battle won, the gypsy gathered up the monstrous heads, buried them in the sand and pressed a rock above them. Then, marching up to the tower, he told the trembling princess, "Go and tell your father it was the three foreign knights that rescued you."

Before running off, the eldest princess took a precious ring

13

from her finger and slipped it on his hand; and as she departed he sought out the three bold men and told them likewise, "I need no royal favors; go to the palace and say it was you who vanquished the sea monster."

To mark the courageous deed, a grand feast was held within the royal halls: the three foreign knights were given seats of honor and showered with praise and treasure by the Czar.

So time went on, and finally the day dawned when the second princess had to fulfil her appointment with the beast. This time the hinny came running to its master, saying, "The second sea monster is more dreadful than the first. Fear not, though, you will conquer if you're bold."

The second princess was borne down to the shore, set in the tower and abandoned to her fate. Once again those bold knights sat waiting, this time behind a hill. Yet the moment a nine-headed serpent appeared on shore, they all turned and fled.

As the monster approached the tower, however, up galloped the hinny and down leapt the sheep's-head gypsy to face his foe.

"Who goes there?" snarled the monster in a terrifying voice.

"You don't scare me," said the gypsy boldly. "I'm going to chop off all nine of your heads!"

And indeed, with his trusty blade the gypsy cut off three monstrous heads at once; but he could not avoid the blows that thrust him waist-deep into the sand. Yet again he swung his sword and another three heads flew off. But this time the monster struck him so hard he sank right up to his neck.

"Hey, monster," the gypsy cried in desperation, "watch out for the three bold knights eager to cut off your three last heads."

As the monster wheeled about to face new foes, the bold knights took to their heels beneath the baleful stare. That

14

gave the gypsy time to scramble up and cut off the three last heads. Gathering up the remains, he buried all nine heads in the selfsame grave beneath the rock. Then he hastened to free the princess and tell her this, "Go to your father and tell him it was the three bold knights who saved you. Not a word of me."

With her deepest thanks, the princess handed him her necklace and hurried off, and he concealed it in his curly hair beneath the sheepskin fleece. When he reached the trembling knights, he told them, "I need no royal blessing; go to the palace and take the praise yourselves."

Once again the banquet hall rang to great rejoicing, and again all praised the valiant knights. Time went on and dark destiny stood once more at the gates: the youngest princess was to wed the twelve-headed sea monster, the strongest and ugliest of all.

And the hinny told its master, "All that has passed till now is only half the fight; you'll find the last monster a much tougher foe. Only with my aid will you defeat him: strike where I stamp my hoof."

But now things took a different turn: those bold knights from overseas plotted to do away with Know Not How, the strange hero in the sheepskin.

"What if he tells tales on us?" they said.

"The Czar would reclaim his gifts!"

"Let's put a sleep charm on him; then the monster will slay him as he sleeps."

No sooner said than done. They crept up on the gypsy as he slept and drugged him with a sleeping spell. So, as Know Not How met the young princess upon the shore, he could barely keep his eyes open.

"I feel so sleepy," he murmured to her. "Wake me when the monster comes."

So saying he dropped his head upon the princess' lap and fell into a slumber.

15

As he slept on, the princess stroked his sheep's head and — well I never! — the fleece fell from his head to reveal black gypsy curls beneath. Seeing one sister's necklace about his neck and the other's ring upon his finger, she guessed at once that it was he who had saved her sisters. And putting the fleece back on his head, she sat and waited.

Suddenly, the sea surged, the water seethed, and out of the waves came the terrible twelve-headed monster. At once she went to wake the gypsy lad, but no matter how much she shook him, even pricked him with a pin, nothing would bring him to. The foreign sleeping charm had taken hold.

Meanwhile, the monster was coming closer and closer, almost now at the tower door; in panic the princess gave way to despair and wept bitter tears.

As the first hot tear fell upon his face, it burnt him more strongly than the fire's flame. In an instant, he was awake — just in the nick of time!

He leapt down from the tower to face the dreadful monster and there began a battle to the death. No sooner had he cut off one head than another grew in its place. Thus they would have grappled on until the monster won had not the hinny intervened. Galloping up it stamped its hoof upon the monster's tail, shouting, "Strike here, here, with all your force!"

At once the gypsy cut through the tail in a single blow; and no fresh heads replaced the old. So he was able to strike off the rest, each and every one, twelve in all. His task complete, the hero ran to the tower, freed the princess and implored her, "Pray, go to your father and tell him the foreign knights slew the beast."

So saying he set to gathering up the monster's heads and burying them beneath a heavy stone along with the other remains. Then he caught up with the fleeing knights who shivered and shook before the valiant man.

"You thought I'd be slain?" he said. "Fear not, I shall spare

16

you. Go to the Czar and say you overcame the beast."

Relieved, the knights scurried to the palace as fast as their legs could carry them. And another mighty feast began, the grandest the world had seen. All the bigwigs and notables were there, all except the sheepskin cook, who was quite cast out of mind. But not by the youngest princess who had seen his face and fallen in love with the handsome gypsy.

"Father," she said, "I would like to invite the gypsy cook to our feast."

"I am afraid, dear daughter, he would offend our guests by his odd appearance."

She begged her father to change his mind and, finally, Know Not How was summoned, seated in a corner and served with the meanest fare.

While the feast was in full swing, the guests set to questioning the knights: how had they dealt with the beasts? And those bold souls, nothing daunted, tried to outdo one another in boasting of their prowess. Growing impatient with these falsehoods, the young princess abruptly asked, "Will you not show our guests where the heads now lie?"

Unwillingly, the knights led the company down to the shore. Having seen where the gypsy had placed the heads, they pointed out the rock at once.

"Show us," continued the young princess, "the monstrous heads so that we all can see how brave you are."

The three knights approached the rock, yet no matter how hard they pushed and shoved, they could not move it. It was then that Know Not How stepped forward, thrust the knights aside and, with one hand, pushed it over as if it were as light as dandelion fluff. Then he dug up the heads and displayed them to the Czar.

How cross the monarch was. He reclaimed all the treasure he'd granted to the cowardly knights, cursing them roundly, "I was even going to wed you to my daughters, you scoundrels.

Guards, drive these brigands from my sight!"

Turning to his daughters, the Czar asked each in turn, "Which of you will marry this bold young man?"

The eldest princess turned her head: what girl would wed a man with ram's horns and eyes?

The second princess likewise turned away in disgust.

"Pray, pardon, sire, we cannot," they exclaimed.

"And you, my youngest daughter?" asked the Czar.

Shyly gazing down, she murmured low, "I'll wed him straightaway."

Thereupon she went up to the gypsy lad and removed the fleece. The crowd all gasped at the sight: a gypsy more handsome than words can tell.

Readily the Czar gave his blessing to the pair, and thenceforth they lived in wealth and cheer for many a long and happy year. Oh yes, lest you forget, for sure the gypsy lad did not: his hinny lived in clover till the end of his days.

BROKEN BEADS

Two gypsy tribes were traveling the world; one was rich, the other poor. And it happened that a boy from the poor tribe fell in love with a girl from the rich tribe. She, too, loved him more than life itself. So they pledged to wed.

Matchmakers went forth to the wealthy gypsies in the time-honored gypsy fashion, bearing a birch branch in their hands; the branch was garlanded in ribbons and ruble notes, ready to lay before the girl's father. But the branch was not accepted: it was snapped in two and cast away.

"I'll find a rich husband for my daughter," the rich man shouted, "not a ragamuffin from your tribe."

The girl threw herself at her father's feet, begging him to take pity on her, not to part her from her beloved; but he would not hear of it, shouted even more furiously, snatched up his whip and lashed her till she was half dead.

"I'll knock all thought of that gypsy out of you," he cried.

Thereafter the couple began to meet secretly. What else would you expect? And they made up their minds to run away.

One dark night the lad crept into the wealthy camp, stole a brace of fine steeds, hitched them to a trap and, with his gypsy lass beside him, away they went – you couldn't see them for dust!

The girl's father ranted and raved. He would not even hear his daughter's name spoken; nor would he receive his errant son-in-law when he later came to seek a pardon. Since the pair had flouted gypsy law they could not return now to either tribe. So they had to wander alone.

Do you know what it means to travel the road alone? Perish the thought. When all are together, look about and you breathe easier, look about and there's a helping hand. But all alone, and poor as well, it's a rotten life. Full one day, belly aching the next.

What was worse, it was approaching autumn, just as the chill got to the bones. For a while the couple managed to live on the edge of a village in a rented hut. They sold the trap and pair, but the money soon gave out, stocks ran low, and they became desperate for food. There was nothing for it but to steal to live. Leaving his wife, the young gypsy set out to try his luck some twenty miles away.

"How will we survive?" he wondered as he trudged along. "Not a penny to our name, no tent, no friends, no gypsies to take us in."

Amidst such gloomy thoughts he suddenly spotted horses grazing in a meadow, and not a soul in sight.

"Look sharp!" he thought. "I'll earn a penny or two at the market, enough to tide us over winter."

No sooner said than done. He crept up on the horses and was just about to grab a stallion when, calamity! From out of nowhere leapt a shepherd, gun cocked.

Bang, bang, bang!

He emptied the gun into the gypsy and killed him stone dead.

When the deed was known, the gypsy girl buried her husband, cut off her plaits and put them on his coffin.

"Grieve not, my darling," she wailed, "I'll come to you soon."

Each day when she went to her husband's grave, she wept and lamented. But you cannot live in grief forever, and one fine day she went no more to the graveyard.

That night, as she made ready for bed, she happened to

glance out of the window and noticed a shadow moving across the yard. Then came footsteps on the porch . . . The door swung open and there stood her husband, as young and handsome as ever. He came in, stoked up the stove and put the kettle on to boil. They drank tea and went to bed.

When she awoke next morning he was gone. From that time on, however, the night repeated itself: at precisely five minutes to midnight her husband came to her and she awaited him. The kettle boiled, the stove was stoked, they drank tea and went to bed.

It was not long before the neighbors began to notice how tired and haggard the poor gypsy woman was.

"What has happened? You get thinner every day," said the old dames.

And she told them her story.

"Your husband surely doesn't come to you!" they gasped. "Maybe you should go to see the village sage? She's wise and knows all there is to know. She'll tell you what to do."

"Please leave me in peace," she said. "I'm quite content."

But her neighbors would not leave her be and finally took her by force to the wise woman, who told her this, "Your husband has become an evil spirit. But don't worry, I'll save you from him. Just draw a cross above your door. He won't dare cross the threshold then."

"I cannot do that," cried the gypsy woman in alarm. "If he stops coming I'll die of despair."

So saying she returned home; yet her neighbors secretly took a piece of charcoal and drew crosses on all her doors.

Night fell. Midnight came but no gypsy. Meanwhile his widow sat waiting: the kettle boiled over, the stove was red hot . . . Then suddenly it was like a stone through the window! Glass flew everywhere and the gypsy's face appeared, black with rage, sparks flying from his eyes, his hair standing on end.

"What a way to greet your husband!" he exclaimed. "Gather up your things at once."

The poor girl was very frightened; she felt that if she left with him now she would never return.

"Just a moment, dear," she murmured. "I have some hot water ready to take a bath; I won't be long."

The gypsy frowned, but did not object. So she washed herself, then set to gathering up her things and putting on her clothes. She dressed herself in a great bundle of clothes, then delved into a chest where she kept her jewelry, and started collecting her beads and earrings.

"What are you up to?" shouted her husband impatiently. "Hurry up, we must be on our way."

"Just a moment, darling, let me put on my mother's beads."

"Why have you put on so many sweaters?"

"How cold it is outside, listen to the wind."

"Don't worry, I'll warm you up," he yelled. "It's as hot as hell in my home."

After a while they emerged together, heading into a howling wind; the trees bent low to the ground, the last leaves swirled about, black storm clouds blocked the moon. It was so dark you could not see a hand before your face.

Upon the road a pair of horses stood between the shafts of a carriage, and what strange steeds they were! She'd never seen the like: their coats gleamed like fire, sparks flew from their eyes. And as soon as they took their seats, the gypsy whistled and the horses raced forward at a mad gallop.

When the moon peeped from behind a cloud, the gypsy girl noticed the horses were not galloping along the road at all, they were flying in the air! Meanwhile her husband was sitting in front, singing merrily at the top of his voice,

"The crescent moon's shining in the sky,
The dead man and wife go riding by."

23

On they went, the girl now almost dead with fright. But the gypsy sang even louder,

> "The crescent moon's shining in the sky,
> The dead man and wife go riding by."

Finally he pulled up his horses at the graveyard gates, gave a whistle and the horses disappeared. He led his wife past tombstones through the graveyard until they reached an open grave. Springing into the muddy pit, he cried, "Come on, hurry up, throw in your clothes and jump in."

"This is the end," she thought.

But she dallied as best she could: slowly she took off each item of clothing, handing it, neatly folded, to her husband. First a headscarf, then a second, first a sweater, then a second. And all as slow as slow could be . . .

"What are you doing?" cried the gypsy from the grave. "Get a move on!"

Just then the girl's beads burst from her neck – secretly she had snapped the thread and now the beads had scattered everywhere.

"Oh dear, oh dear," she moaned, "Dear husband, I cannot come without my mother's beads."

On hands and knees she set to picking up her beads. One bead – over to her husband, and a second, third, fourth, and so on. She would not be satisfied until every single bead was recovered. By that time dawn's early light streaked the sky, and the very edge of the forest glimmered white.

"Jump in!" shrieked the gypsy frantically.

"Coming," she called. "Just my earrings left . . ."

She dropped one earring into the grave and was about to take off the other when the gypsy lunged forward to pull her in. As she leapt back she heard the third cockcrow ring out. The gypsy gnashed his teeth, groaned loudly, gave a wild

24

shriek and fell back into the grave. As the coffin lid banged shut, earth flew on to it and a grave mound formed of its own accord.

The poor girl fell to the ground in a dead faint.

How long she lay there she did not recall, but when she came to she was stark naked, apart from one earring clenched in a fist. With one fearful glance at the grave, she dashed helter-skelter for the graveyard chapel, climbed up to the bell tower and rang the bells for all she was worth. Folk came running from all directions, the old priest as well.

What a sight met their eyes! The naked gypsy girl swinging on the bell rope . . . She was quickly brought clothing and helped down; then she recounted her story to the astounded crowd. After leading them to her husband's grave, she clawed at the earth with her bare hands to show them what lay beneath . . .

The gypsy lay face down, and all around him was his wife's clothing, crumpled and torn, and beads all strewn about. The priest sprinkled holy water on the upturned earth and an aspen stake was hammered into the grave.

Since then no more gypsy ghosts have appeared in the graveyard.

SAINT GEORGE AND THE GYPSIES

One time Saint George was riding along when he came upon a gypsy trailer. A nut-brown gypsy was sitting in the riding seat pulling on the reins.

"Where are you bound for, gypsy?" asked Saint George.

"Where the wind blows," the gypsy replied. "And you?"

"Jerusalem. To see how the Good Lord fares."

"Good fellow," said the gypsy, "spare us a thought, us gypsies. Tell the Lord that we wander the land. Let Him tell us how to live."

"Very well," replied Saint George. "I'll bring you God's word on my return."

"You'll forget us," said the gypsy, shaking his head.

"No, as God's my witness, I won't forget."

Gazing at Saint George's mount, the gypsy saw it was a thoroughbred, with a gold harness studded with precious stones, its stirrup of pure gold.

"I'll tell you what, brother," said the gypsy, "leave me your harness; then you'll remember gypsies every time you mount your steed."

"You're a crafty one," said Saint George with a grin. "All right, I'll leave you my harness; only mark this: I want it back on my return."

"How could you doubt me?" the gypsy said scornfully.

On that they parted. Off went Saint George, on and on until

he passed through a village and came upon some peasants felling timber for a house. He could see the logs were not long enough to make a wall. The peasants had tied ropes and were tugging hard at those logs from both ends, trying to stretch them. Amazed at this, Saint George rode up and asked, "What are you up to, peasants?"

"It's like this, master, the logs are a bit short, so we have to stretch them. But the stubborn devils won't give. Perhaps you can tell us what to do?"

"In your place I would saw more wood, but I'll ask God if you like. I'm on my way to Jerusalem now."

The peasants were delighted.

As Saint George rode on he came upon two wells, with women carrying pails on yokes between them: they took water from one well and poured it into the other. As he came in view, the women called him over.

"Hey there, handsome! Where are you bound?"

"To Jerusalem, to pay my respects to God."

"Oi, dearie!" they cried. "Ask the Lord to take pity on us. How much longer must we pour water from one well into the other?"

Saint George agreed, rode on and finally came to Jerusalem for an audience with the Lord. He first asked after His health, then ventured to ask about the peasants stretching logs.

"I know all about that," said God. "It's I who made them stupid for being so mean and sly. They intended to build a house as well as put by logs for winter – that's what they get for being mean and stupid. You tell those peasants, George, that I forgive them their sins, but they must be kind and wise in future."

"I saw another marvel," continued Saint George. "Women were pouring water from one well into another."

"I know all about that, too," said God. "I punished them for watering the milk they sold in town. And I'll pardon them

27

as long as they mend their ways."

"I'll pass the message on," said the Saint.

He was just about to mount his horse when his foot slipped and he all but took a tumble – at once he recalled the gypsies.

"I almost forgot, God help me. I promised to ask you how gypsies are to live."

"Tell the gypsies this," said God. "Let them live by their own laws. Where they pray, where they beg, where they take without leave – that's their affair. Tell them that."

Saint George set off on his return. He met the women, told them what God had said and – slit my throat and hope to die! – they'd never water the milk again.

Saint George arrived at the village where the peasants were still trying to stretch the logs, and told them of God's word: He forgave them, but no more scrounging! Overjoyed, the peasants set about their task with wiser heads.

On went Saint George and eventually came to the gypsy camp. As he rode in, little gypsies hopped around him, crying, "Saint George is here, Saint George is here."

The adults gathered round.

"Well, what does God say of us?" asked the selfsame gypsy.

"Listen closely: where you pray, where you beg, where you take without leave – that's up to you."

"Thank God He did not forget the gypsies," they all cried.

"As for you, gypsy," said Saint George to the man he'd met before, "give back my harness, as you said."

"What harness? Good God, I took no harness from you, upon my soul. Oh no, no, no. Let the moon cut me down if I tell a lie. May my children see no happiness if I ever robbed you!"

So the gold harness stayed with the gypsies. After all, God did say it was up to them where they prayed, where they begged and where they took without leave.

THE OUTCAST

Down through the ages the meeting of gypsy tribes has not always been friendly. If two camps of different tribes meet, don't expect sweetness and honey; tribes have long been hostile to one another.

One time a gypsy from the Lovary tribe fell in love with a girl from the Servo clan. What could he do? He was determined to marry her, but how could he go against the gypsy word? Finally, he went to tell his problems to the chieftain, but the old man would not listen.

"You cannot go against gypsy law," was all he said.

"To hell with the law that spoils our happiness," retorted the gypsy angrily.

That set the whole camp muttering against him.

"How dare he spit on gypsy law!"

"It's a wonder the earth does not strike him down!"

"Since he thinks thus," said the gypsy chieftain, holding up his hand for silence, "we need him no more. Leave him be, let him learn what it is to be alone."

Having spoken, the chieftain motioned the gypsies to gather up their things and take to the road, abandoning the hot-headed gypsy.

Once alone, the gypsy could not understand at all. He glanced from the whip tightly clenched in his hand to the branches above; he sank to his knees to blow on the dying embers of the fire. Yet the fire had no will to live. After a while the gypsy grew afraid and ran in pursuit of the departing tribe. He ran in panic, his lungs bursting, often tripping over and full of dread, pulling himself up and rushing on; he stuck fast to the narrow rut made by the gypsy wagons.

Only at dawn, as he reached a river bank, did he see his gypsy band at rest. Beside a tent on the high river-bank by a fading fire sat an old man, smoking a pipe and gazing at the shadows darting across the ground.

"Old man," cried the outcast, "was the chieftain right to drive me out for love? Is it my fault the girl and I are from different tribes?'

The old fellow sat silent. He did not even glance toward the gypsy, just continued puffing on his pipe and staring into the embers.

In his anger the young gypsy began to curse the world: the chieftain for driving him out, the gypsy girl who could not be his, the gypsies for their unfair laws . . .

"Old man, surely you know I'm right," he cried. "You're just scared of going against gypsy law."

Finally the old man broke his silence, "You broke gypsy law three times. You cursed your brothers who nurtured you; you cursed the fire that warmed you; you cursed the one you love. Are you not worthy of your punishment?"

"You cannot punish a man for love!"

"You are not punished for love, but for hate."

"Hate . . ." the old man quietly repeated.

And in the moonlight a knife flashed and entered the heart of the headstrong gypsy.

VASYA WHITEFEET

There was once a wealthy gypsy who was master of forests, pastures and villages; and he had an only son – Vasya, nicknamed Whitefeet. How did his nickname arise?

Now, as you know, all gypsies are born dark-skinned. Yet this lad was as white as snow, not gypsy-like at all; so folk called him Vasya Whitefeet.

In time the old gypsy died and left Vasya a rich inheritance. Not only was he now a wealthy man, he was also wise and handsome. On his twentieth birthday he went to his mother and said, "Mother, we need for nothing, know no misfortune, and live in comfort. I wish to know how other gypsies live. I want to travel about the world, take a look at people, learn about life."

His mother did not argue; he spoke the truth.

"Go, my son," she said, "learn from people how to make a living."

So Vasya Whitefeet changed into shabby clothes, took an old oilskin as leaky as a sieve, two penny coins and a stale crust of bread, and took to the road.

In time he arrived at a gypsy camp with fine tents standing, horses grazing in the meadow, camp fires crackling, gypsy women singing songs and the menfolk deep in conversation.

Acting the fool, Vasya made his way towards the gypsy fire. Where he had been white before he was now as black as the ace of spades, having covered himself with mud on the way. A

31

proper *Calo Rom*! Black Gypsy! So the gypsy clan took him for a harmless fool who would give them some amusement.

From then on if a gypsy poked fun at anyone it would be poor Vasya: what a buffoon he was!

One evening the gypsies were gathered round the fire, singing and dancing; one played the accordion, one the guitar. And Vasya whispered in the accordionist's ear, "Hey, *mora*, give us a go. I fancy squeezing out a tune."

"But can you play, Vasenka?" the fellow asked. "You don't want folk laughing at you, do you?"

"How do I know I can play or not until I try?" he giggled stupidly.

That set the gypsies off. "Go on, give him a try."

With a knowing wink the accordionist lifted the instrument from his shoulders and passed it to Vasya. And the lad circled the fire, his fingers tripping lightly over the buttons, making such a catchy gypsy tune that he set their feet a'tapping and their tongues a'wagging. Well I never! – who'd have thought it?

From then on Vasya became a favorite in the camp. By day not a scrap of notice, but by night, when the camp-fire circle was complete, it was, "Come on Vasya. Good old Vasya!"

All the same, he continued to act the fool, living under his oilskin slung above a bush, with the bare earth for a mattress, a coat for a blanket, his boots for a pillow.

One day the word went round that a rich wedding was to be held in the neighborhood, that matchmakers had come for the wealthy Rosa whose beauty was known throughout the district. And it was also said behind the hand, in whispers, that Rosa was not partial to her future groom. But her father was unyielding.

Next morning Vasya rose before the rest and set off home. Coming to his mother, he ordered, "Here, Ma! Fetch out my Sunday best: the brocade shirt, Moroccan boots and the finest horse. I'd better take a wash as well."

32

"What's all this for, son?" she asked.

"Fair Rosa's father is to wed her to an old widower. Maybe I'll save her the trouble: I'll just take a look to see if she's as pretty as they say."

"Do as you wish, son," his mother said. "But beware of Rosa's father: a gypsy father's word should not be crossed."

Vasya set off for Rosa's camp, taking with him his favorite fiddle. When he arrived he saw a host of guests gathered for the wedding; and they were delighted to have him play his fiddle.

The tunes his fiddle played were tender and sad, so moving that Rosa wept as if only now fully realizing her bitter fate. Staring at the fiddler, her heart overflowed. Such a smart, handsome fellow. Meanwhile, the guests walked about gossiping, supping and drinking, with no more thought for bride and groom. Choosing his moment, Vasya Whitefeet stole up to Rosa and whispered in her ear, "I can see you don't love the man they've chosen for you. Dear Rosa, let's run away together; you broke my heart the moment I set eyes on you."

Rosa was silent, she just gave him a look that said it all. And they made off secretly together.

The camp would have made merry till morning, not noticing the escape, had the groom not had to carry off the bride, by gypsy custom.

What a rumpus – Rosa's gone! And the fiddler too! Rosa's father flew into a rage, sent a hundred riders in pursuit of the fleeing pair – but there was no catching Vasya. He brought Rosa home to his mother.

"This is my bride," he announced. "Love her as your own dear daughter."

"Very well, son," his mother said, "though my heart aches; can we not have a proper gypsy wedding?"

"Certainly," he cried. "Only I must invite my gypsy friends."

Next morning Vasya Whitefeet donned his tattered rags, rolled around in the dust, and made for the gypsy encampment. As he arrived the camp was buzzing with the news; some bold Rom had carried off Rosa right under the bridegroom's nose.

"Now then, Vasya, maybe you know who spoiled Rosa's wedding night?" the gypsies joked.

"I do and all," he said. "It was me."

That set the gypsies off in helpless laughter.

"Oh-ho-ho! Oh-ho-ho! You don't mean to say . . ."

"What did you carry her off on – Shanks's pony?"

"Perhaps she fancies sleeping under a bush?"

The jokes came thick and fast.

"Go on, brothers, laugh away," said Vasya with a smile. "And when you've done put on your glad rags and come to my wedding."

"Where's that? Under your oilskin?" they cried.

"At my wealthy friend's. He has a good spread a mile off, all plush and marble. Plenty to eat, and wine to wash it down."

"So, *Romaly*," spoke up the camp elder, "we've nothing to lose: if this dolt lies, we'll tan his hide; if not we'll enjoy a feed. Let's go."

And the men of the camp set off. Vasya Whitefeet marched ahead, the others followed some way behind. He led them to his own house. As he was nearing home, he dashed on ahead, washed and changed his clothes – you'd never have recognized the fair young lad sparkling like a new pin. Then out he came to greet the gypsy band.

"Are you the gypsies Vasya invited?" he asked the chief.

"We are that. Where's Vasya?" the man replied.

"Come on in, *chiavalei*, we've been expecting you."

Entering the yard, the gypsies saw a fire blazing, and each was led to his own fireside place, given a smart new change of

34

clothes: a suit of cloth, silk shirt, velvet cap – all fitted like a dream. Then each gypsy was scrubbed, shaved and tidied up, with the old men's beards trimmed just right. You'd have thought they were townsfolk, not wandering gypsies.

When all was ready, the gypsies took their places at the table, gasping at the wealth of food – all their bellies could contain.

In the midst of the feast, Vasya stood up and announced, "Now then, *chiavalei*, raise your glasses to the bride and groom: fair Rosa and Vasya Whitefeet!"

"Say, where's this pal of yours, Vasya Whitefeet?" called a gypsy. "I don't see him anywhere."

Thereupon, Vasya approached the camp musician, took the accordion from his hands and began to play. The moment his fingers touched the buttons there flowed such lively gypsy melodies . . .

At once the gypsies realized whose home this was. Shiver and shake, they all but dropped their glasses.

"So you, you . . . must be Vasya Whitefeet!"

"Fear not, friends," he said smiling. "You never did me harm. You fed me, took me in, even though I was a fool. And I can pardon your jokes: fun makes you forget your cares and woes."

For three whole days, the gypsies celebrated, and on the fourth they hitched up their horses and returned home. And when they packed up their camp and traveled on, Rosa and Vasya remained in their fine house.

One week went by, and then the next. And Vasya's feet began to itch.

"What's the matter, husband mine?" asked Rosa.

"All a man could desire is mine," he replied. "Yet after living with those gypsies, some restless spirit seems to call me to the open road, to sit beside the gypsy fire and hear a gypsy song . . ."

"To tell you truly," she said, "the settled life is not for me either."

It was agreed. Next day they loaded up three horses and set off in a wagon to overtake the departed clan.

One evening at dusk, shortly after, the gypsies noticed a cloud of dust fast approaching along the road; it sent them rushing about their tents.

"The district police! Run for it, lads!"

Yet as they peered from their tents, relief and delight filled their hearts as Vasya and Rosa appeared; and the gypsies poured out to make them welcome. From then on Rosa and Vasya never parted company with the gypsy clan. And when the elder died, the gypsies chose Vasya Whitefeet to lead them on their way.

GYPSIES WHO ALL BUT CHEATED THEMSELVES

There were once two brother gypsies who lived by craft and guile. They owned a jet-black stallion – no ordinary steed. As the brothers went about their business, that horse could sense danger a mile off. If it stamped the ground, that spelt trouble. So whenever they were on a job, they left the stallion on the road and kept close watch on it.

One time they thought to rob a merchant, left their stallion close by, and crept towards a barn. Unfortunately for them, a massive old padlock hung from the barn door, and there was no way in.

"Know what, brother?" whispered one, "Let's dig a tunnel beneath the door."

The tunnel was duly dug and, while one crawled into the barn, the other stood guard, ready to receive the booty.

Now, good folk, you should know that every barn has its goblin. You don't know what a goblin is? Well, he can take any form – human, bird or animal – and he lives in the farmyard protecting the animals. If he takes to a horse, fancies its color or something else, he'll protect it himself, brushing its mane and coat until they gleam, and its eyes are bright and keen. The goblin always pets his favorites, gives them fond pats. And you don't have to feed such animals – their bellies are full without your fodder.

But if he takes a dislike to any beast, sell it forthwith or he'll drive it round the yard, torment it until tears roll down its muzzle. He might even set to tickling the poor beasts, and that will make them mad, foam at the mouth, choke and die.

You have to respect the goblin, bring him bread and salt – he adores respect. Of an evening, as the sun goes down, you must go into the yard to pay your respects, say this, that and the other – "Dear Master Goblin," "regards to your children," "do let my horse come quietly" – and you'll have bread and salt a'plenty. And don't forget to bow three times . . .

So now the goblin watched crossly as the gypsy crawled into the barn and set to steal a sheep.

"Hey, gypsy!" the goblin shrieked in rage, "leave that sheep be; if you touch a hair on its back I'll skin you alive."

And they came to blows. Meanwhile the stallion on the road was snorting and stamping as it sensed the danger.

After some time the gypsy emerged from the barn empty-handed – the goblin had got the better of him.

"I put up a fight," he told his brother, "but how can you beat a goblin? He tossed me into the hayloft, and as I slid down he threw me into the food trough; next he hoisted me onto the ram's horns. He shook me and twisted me, I tell you I was lucky to escape."

"Listen, brother," said the other, "my wife tells me they've just slaughtered a hog here, ready for the holiday. Surely the goblin won't be guarding a dead hog?"

"You're right; let's steal the hog."

Both glanced round at their horse – it seemed to be standing quietly now. So they crept towards the outhouse, right by the farmhouse. By now it was so dark you could poke out your eye in the gloom. The outhouse was even worse. At last their fumbling fingers felt the dead carcass of the hog, and they quickly heaved it on to their shoulders and made off with it.

Dropping it into their cart and covering it up with sacking, they made off post-haste.

"Phew!" sighed one, "That's some hog; we barely carried it between us."

"I'm famished after that tussle with the goblin," said the other. "I could do with some roast pork. Let's get a fire going now and fry us some pig."

"Hold on, brother, we'd better be well clear of the village first. Let's wait until we come home and have a good feast there."

By the time they reached home it was quite light, and a crowd of gypsies came out to meet them.

"How did it go, lads?"

"See for yourselves, there's a hog in the cart under the sacking. Let's shift it indoors."

Two strong gypsies went over to the cart, drew aside the sacking and froze in their tracks.

"What's this?" they cried.

Rushing to the cart, the brothers looked in and . . . could not believe their eyes. A dead man lay there, cold and stiff!

What were they to do? It had to be disposed of before the villagers came searching. So they carried it indoors, lay it on the stove, and sat down to think, not daring to glance towards the dead man.

As they were discussing what to do, they suddenly heard a noise from the stove. Staring in disbelief, they saw first an arm and then a leg move. Next one eye opened followed by the second, and both eyes stared round the room.

Gypsies don't scare easily, that's well known, but there was fear now in the room. It dawned on the brothers that the fellow must have been dead drunk and the villagers had taken him for dead, dumping him in his own shed. And they had picked up his body in the dark! Having got over their fear they wondered how they might somehow profit from this error.

Before their eyes the dead man slowly sat up and spoke, "Where am I?"

"You're in hell," the gypsies told him. "We're demons and we're just preparing a pot to roast you in."

"Oh, please don't, dear demons," wailed the man. "I'll make it worth your while . . ."

"Why, do you want to go back to earth?"

"I do, I do, dear demons, there's nothing I wouldn't give."

"Right, let's strike a bargain: we'll take you home, and you reward us well."

The deal was struck. The man was wrapped up again, placed in the cart and driven back to the village. By now the loss had been discovered, and the dead man's household was yelling and wailing. Then all of a sudden the door burst open and in came the gypsies carrying the dead body.

"You bandits, grave-robbers!" yelled the peasants. "You can't even leave the dead in peace!"

"Hold your shouting and take a look," the gypsies said.

As the sacking was drawn back, the "dead" man sat up. What a hullabaloo! Some fainted clean away; but the "dead" master of the house rewarded the gypsy demons well, giving them the very sheep they had earlier tried to steal.

"That's for delivering me from Hell," he said.

So you see, wonders abound . . . if you play your cards right!

THE QUEEN OF SPADES

Gypsy women are great fortune-tellers; that is well known. But they tell fortunes in different ways: some on the palm, some by cards, when you want to know the future. But there are some who consult the devil, and that needs caution. It is one step from disaster.

There are also some young gypsy girls who tell fortunes by a mirror or gold ring; that's to find out their future husbands. They wish to see and remember the face that appears – so as not to let fate slip by them unawares. Husband-seeking is usually done on New Year's Eve, when young people get together as soon as the grown-ups are out.

They sit a young girl down at the table, drop a gold ring in a glass of water and turn out the lamp. Then she gazes into the glass, waiting for the face of her future husband to appear in the gold ring.

And another thing. You must not look long at your promised one's face or the devil will have you; the moment you see a face, signal for the lamp to be lit, otherwise . . .

One time some gypsy girls assembled to tell fortunes. It was New Year's Eve, the parents were out, and the tent lamp turned down low. The daughter of the tent sat down at the table, dropped her mother's gold ring into a glass of water, and waited . . . All the girls stood about her waiting, one girl ready to turn up the lamp at a signal.

One hour passed, then another. Nothing. No one appeared. Midnight came and went. Still no husband.

Then all of a sudden, the girl's face turned pale, she could not utter a word, and her head bent nearer and nearer to the glass.

SMACK!

A slap rang out loud and clear. In a flash the lamp was turned up and, in its glow, they saw the poor girl, half-dead with fright, a trickle of blood upon her chin.

It took all their efforts to bring her round. Then came the questions: for heaven's sake, what happened? What did you see?

"At first nothing's happening," she murmured. "Then I see a gleam at the bottom of the glass, I see a swamp, and a big rock in the middle; demons are running round the rock, tiny ones, all leaping about. And the rock's coming closer and closer. Suddenly, the demons disappear, all save one: he climbs on to the rock and stares straight at me. Then his face comes nearer and nearer . . . I can't take my eyes away – it's a human face! That of a young man. And he says to me, he says, 'Come to me, my beauty! Come nearer!'

"He reaches out to me, and he's got long claws on his fingers. Then he digs them into me and pulls me down. Just then comes a crack . . . And I don't remember any more."

So there we are, telling fortunes can be a dangerous business if you don't watch out.

There are also gypsies who tell fortunes by the Queen of Spades. She can tell you about the future, tell you anything, even answer questions. What you have to do is put the card – the Queen of Spades – in the doorway, sit by the door and say,

"Come forth, O Queen, come forth and tell our fortunes."

Oh, and don't forget to place a chair near the door. In comes the Queen of Spades and sits on that chair. That's when you have to ask her about your future. Only for heaven's sake, don't go butting in while she's telling her tale, nor delay her as she leaves.

So one time the gypsies were telling fortunes by the Queen of Spades. It was a merry crew, all youngsters, giggling nervously and not a little scared. They had put the card behind the door, yet had not left enough room for her to pass, though they did not know it at the time.

They sat and waited, but she did not come. Midnight passed and no Queen of Spades; two o'clock and nothing. Till three o'clock in the morning the gypsies waited for the Queen, and she did not appear. Well, you can't wait forever, and they got fed up with waiting, split up and made for home. The lad who lived in the house, however, dallied awhile.

"You go on," he told his friends, "I'll just tidy up and be with you in a minute."

Off the others went and waited for him at the crossroads. It was a frosty night, and they had to stamp their feet to keep warm as they waited. They were just about to go their separate ways when, suddenly, they heard a low groan from down the road. And there was their friend crawling towards them on hands and knees, reaching out to them for help.

Rushing towards him, they picked him up, barely alive: his face was as white as a sheet, his tongue and eyes were poking out. It was dawn before he was able to tell them the story.

"When you had gone, I tidied up and went into the passage to follow, locking the living-room door behind me. Just as I went to open the outside door, there came a pounding from the other side, so violent I thought it would fly off its hinges.

"'Who's there?' I cried. No reply, though the knocking grew

43

even louder. I sprang back just in time. The door caved in and into the passage stepped . . ." The poor lad gave a groan.

"Who? Who was it?"

"THE QUEEN OF SPADES! What a beauty! There she stood in the gloom. I first thought she was wearing a white gown, yet in the moonlight shining through the window it gleamed all black. Tall, too, a good head taller than me; she stood staring at me, silent. Not a word. I was scared stiff.

"Then she came floating towards me ever so slowly, stretching out her arms. If only I could have escaped back into the living-room, but I couldn't find the key in time. I threw myself against the door, but it wouldn't give. And still the Queen came on, her hands almost about my throat. With one last effort I leapt head first through the window, tumbling head over heels into the snow.

"Even then she did not give up: slowly, she floated down the steps and came after me. I pulled myself up and ran stumbling after you. You must have found me in the nick of time . . ."

The lad ended his story. And, believe me, he never tried to summon up the Queen of Spades again.

Be warned: the gypsies say you must be very careful when telling fortunes.

THE GYPSY WHO ALMOST SWAPPED
PLACES WITH A DEVIL

Once there was a gypsy. He had roamed the earth and seen so much of life that nothing scared him at all. And he had the strength of an ox – he would take on bears single-handed and out-wrestle them before sticking his knife into their flesh. But those bears left their marks on him. His entire body was streaked with so many bear scars that he was as black and gruesome as Old Nick himself. All he lacked was a pair of horns.

When he was too old for wandering, he settled in a lone hut at the edge of a village. The villagers would keep out of his way, frightened by his fearsome appearance.

Late one evening, the old gypsy decided to steam himself in the village bath-house; no one would likely be there at that late hour. So, fetching water from the stream, he lit the fire, stretched out on the bath-house shelf and watched the sweat roll down his body. Ah, just the job!

Now, this was round about midnight. And there he was enjoying a good steam, switching his sides and buttocks with oak twigs, when he suddenly heard a voice alongside him.

"Shove over, lad."

He moved along, thinking a villager had joined him; the air was so steamy you couldn't see a thing.

"Sit yourself down," said the gypsy.

"No, no, shift yourself over to the window," droned on the voice.

Somewhat annoyed at this intruder, he nonetheless moved closer to the window.

"Ah, that's better," came the voice. "Right, lad, give us a rub-down. I'm right partial to a good steam."

"Where are you?" muttered the gypsy. "I can't see you in this fug."

"Over here, fellow; here, sitting on the shelf."

Groping his way forward, the old gypsy set to rubbing down his companion, scrubbing him with oak twigs. Not that he had any clear idea whom he was washing.

"Hey, old friend," came the voice again, "chuck some more logs on, let's get a decent steam up, stir the pot!"

That was a bit too much for the gypsy.

"Do it yourself," he shouted. "You come in here, ordering folk about; have respect for your elders."

"Hee-hee," giggled a voice. "Elders? I'm the same age as you."

At that the gypsy lost his temper with the insolent stranger.

"If I could see your face I'd poke my fist in it," he threatened.

"What do you want to see my face for?" chuckled the other. "I look just like you: I'm your double."

"Double? I'll give you double black eyes when I get hold of you!"

The gypsy's companion roared with laughter, so hard it made the bath-house rock. Now the old gypsy began to realize something fishy was afoot. And when he bent down to stir the coals, he saw a figure in the glow and a pair of hairy legs dangling down. But instead of feet the fellow had hoofs!

It was the devil sitting there!

Now the gypsy could see him well: a short stumpy figure with a tail tossed over his shoulder and horns sticking out of his head. That old devil was poking out his tongue and making faces at him. It was Old Nick all right; yet the funny thing was he looked just like the gypsy.

"I hear tell you're a tough 'un," said the devil.

"So what," snarled the gypsy, "d'you want a taste of my strength?"

"Later maybe," sniggered the devil. "For the moment it's my turn to rub you down."

"I know your fiendish rub-downs," exclaimed the gypsy. "To hell with you."

Thereupon the devil jumped down from the shelf, landing astride the gypsy's shoulders, and set to driving the poor fellow round and round the bath-house. He drove him up the spout, pushed him under the bench, dragged him across the coals, all but dumped him in the pot of hot water. And there was nothing the gypsy could do to throw him off.

Finally, the devil grew tired of the game.

"Come on, old timer," he said, "let's have a fight."

How the gypsy was itching to pay the demon back! He readily agreed.

"Only it's too cramped in here, let's find a bit of space outside," he said.

It did not take them long to find a clearing in the woods, and they instantly came to grips. It was just sparring at first, but in no time at all the feathers really flew. Back and forth they tumbled, punching and scratching, pinching and biting. They fought on through the night, but by morning the old gypsy was dead-beat and ready to yield. Thereupon, the devil pulled out one of the gypsy's teeth, crying, "This'll be a token of the battle. From now on, as long as I have this tooth, you'll be my servant."

Boring a hole in the tooth with his nail, the devil threaded it on a horse hair and strung it round his neck. Just at that moment the third cockcrow rang out.

47

"Well, see you, old pal," cried the devil, and disappeared.

Such a hiding had the devil given him that the poor gypsy could not move for hours; as soon as he could he crawled down to the stream to douse himself and bring his body back to life.

Not a word did he say to the villagers about the night just past, and he kept well clear of that bath-house. But from then on the devil gave him no rest; the old joker must have taken a shine to the gypsy, perhaps because they were so alike. Anyway, as soon as night fell, Old Nick would arrive at the gypsy's hut, sit down, drink tea and play a game of cards with him, as if they were the best of friends.

One time the devil said, "Why don't we bet on the cards? You beat me and I'll do your will, if I win you do mine."

So they played a hand or two, and the devil easily outsmarted the gypsy, who now expected some fresh torment.

"Grab yourself a spade and follow me," the devil said.

Obediently, the gypsy picked up his spade, donned his coat and followed the black, hairy figure through the woods, over streams, round gullies and back into the trees. Finally they emerged into a clearing in which there stood a well.

"Down you go, old pal," the devil said, "down into the well and dig. It's quite dry, no water at all. Everything you find is yours."

The gypsy climbed down into the well and began to dig. He had only been at work for a short while when he unearthed several gold coins, enough to fill his pockets. But the devil just laughed.

"There are plenty more of them. Just dig, dig, dig."

From then on the gypsy was rich. He built himself a new hut, bought a fine brace of steeds, and lived in luxury.

Every night, however, he accompanied the devil to the golden well and – wonders will never cease, dug up as many coins as his pockets would hold! He dug by night and slept by day.

One afternoon he had a dream. He saw the devil and his grandmother deep in conversation. And this is what he heard: "How long before you swap places with the gypsy?" the old hag was saying.

"This very night he'll reach my old clay pipe," replied the devil. "The moment he takes a puff of that pipe he'll be chained to the well for good, with horns, hoofs and long black tail for company."

The gypsy woke up in a sweat, hollering out, "Ah you horned devil, so that's your game! Just you wait, I'll get the better of you yet."

Midnight came and the devil appeared, led the gypsy through the trees to the golden well and lowered him down on a rope. Within a few minutes the gypsy was clambering out again.

"What's the matter?" asked the devil in surprise.

"What do you expect?" said the gypsy. "I've been digging for a month or more, and now the rope's too short."

Scratching his head at this unexpected twist, the devil muttered, "What are we going to do?"

"Simple. Take the horse hair from your neck, plait it into the rope and it'll do just nicely."

With a wary glance at the gypsy, the devil untied the horse hair from his neck and handed it over, tooth and all. At once the old gypsy tied the hair to the rope and lowered himself down into the well once more. Now he was free of the devil's power.

He had only dug a few more spadefuls of earth when he came upon a pipe, and no ordinary smoker's pipe: it was shaped like the devil! Instead of eyes it had sapphires sparkling with fire, like a sly grinning demon. With the pipe in his hand, the gypsy hauled himself back up the well.

"Hey, devil," he called, "come and take a look at this."

"Hey, that's just what we need!" shouted the devil, barely

49

able to conceal his joy. "Let's have a good smoke."

They lit a fire, sat round it and the devil filled the pipe with tobacco from his pouch; this he handed to the gypsy.

"Here, old friend, you take first pull."

Unbeknown to the devil, the gypsy sprinkled some birch dust on top and lit up; now the pipe smoldered and smoked while the gypsy just pretended to take deep pulls.

"This tobacco's a mite strong for me," he said coughing and handing the pipe to his companion.

With a guffaw, the devil took a long pull on the pipe and smiles of pleasure wrinkled his black hairy face.

"Thought you had me there, didn't you?" cried the gypsy to the devil.

And he leapt upon him, tied him up with the rope and left him bound hand and foot. Then he tossed the pipe into the flames – and as it burnt, so the devil faded with it. And he was never seen again.

As for the gypsy, he returned home happily, lived out his years and never set eyes on any devil till the very end of his days.

THE ADVENTURES OF PICHTA, HELADO AND BOTA

In an ancient city of our Russia, let us say Moscow, there dwelt a gypsy by the name of Pichta. His fame had spread to many parts of the land, the gypsies everywhere spoke well of him; he lived a life of ease, though he had never once stolen from a soul.

Pichta lived a settled life, dealing in horses; he sold to merchants, traded at fairs and horse bazaars. That's how he made his fortune. And he lived in peace and comfort with his wife Ruby.

Meanwhile, some way off, there were two brothers living in a gypsy camp. The elder was Helado, the younger Bota. And those two brothers gained a reputation by their robbing skill. They would take whole herds of horses, pick clean villages and stores, yet never once get caught.

One time the brothers drove their horses to a fair, made a good profit and entered a tavern to drink to their good fortune.

"Say, brother Helado," said the younger. "What fame we enjoy amongst gypsies! You won't find a Romany on earth who is our equal."

"Oi, oi, little brother!" the elder said, "is that truly fame? Now, I've heard of a gypsy, Pichta, who dwells in Moscow. He lives ten times better than us, yet does not steal at all."

"Well, what are we waiting for? Let's pay him a visit. Let's see whether he's as rich and famous as they say."

No sooner said than done. The brothers saddled horses, harnessed a cart full of merchandise, and made tracks for Moscow. As they approached the city, they asked people where the gypsy Pichta had his home. And all good bodies, young and old, showed them the way. The brothers were amazed. So they rode on unerringly to Pichta's house.

Now you should know, good folk, that when a gypsy meets a gypsy, hospitality must be shown, however modest. Guests must be respected: give them a crust of bread even if it is your last; give them a corner to bed down in for the night.

So when the brothers entered, Pichta straightaway sat them down at the table and began to treat them well. Talk flowed out of the wine. And what is the first question gypsies ask?

"What gypsies are you? What is your tribe?" asked Pichta. (That's how gypsies come to know each other.)

"Well, *mora*, have you heard of two brothers, Helado and Bota, they who have been stealing all their lives and were never caught?"

"That I have," said Pichta. "Surely, more than once. Those gypsies have a fine reputation."

"That's us. We've come to pay you a call, since your reputation is greater even than ours."

The moment Pichta learned what guests he was entertaining, he ordered his men to rouse the serving maid and set the finest table. And feasting began.

What do gypsies talk about at table?

Those who deal with horses talk of horses, horse fairs, horse prices and such like, while those who steal turn the talk to stealing. So the brothers talked of their noble trade. Pichta listened patiently, then said, "Listen, *chiavalei*, I know a place. Take my word, you and your children could live in clover for the rest of your lives."

52

Now, tell a thief a story and do you think he'll let it go? Not on your life. The brothers peppered Pichta with questions.

"What place?" (Only you don't ask straight out, you creep up on it.)

Being crafty, the brothers knew that if you ask straight out, say, where you can lay your hands on a fortune, no one will tell. So they twisted the conversation this way and that, then finally asked right out, "So, uh, *mora*, where exactly is this fortune stowed?"

"Why, here in the city," Pichta replied. "I'll show you if you like. We'll go just as soon as it gets dark and the coast is clear."

Night fell. The brothers could not sit still, so eager were they get to work.

"Right, lads," said Pichta at last, "take a sack each and let's get cracking."

They each took a sack and went into the dark, unfamiliar city; the brothers had no idea where Pichta was taking them. Imagine their shock when they found themselves outside an old church.

"Where have you led us?" they exclaimed in horror.

"There's enough gold in this church to last for ten lives. You can take just as much as you can carry."

Helado and Bota halted in their tracks.

"Now look here, *mora*, we won't rob a church. Slit our throats, we won't! Tell us to rob a mother of her baby, we'll do it. But not a church!"

In those days, you see, there was a law: if a thief was caught about his trade, he would be sent to jail or exiled to Siberia, but if he was nabbed in church, right away, without court, no fuss – rope about the neck. Execution was the only judge. So no matter what Pichta said, the brothers just replied, "no," "no," "no." At length Pichta lost patience and made for the doors alone.

"What sort of crooks are you?" he shouted. "Here am I, never robbed in my life. I'm game, but you . . . What a miserable pair!"

What could they do? They had to go along.

The three of them first broke the heavy padlock and opened the church doors. Pichta lit some candles and set about stuffing gold ornaments into his sack. He knew where the gold lay, having seen it many times whilst about his business at church.

And all would have gone well had all three filled their sacks without delay, but the brothers were so scared they dithered and clanged, and the watchman raised the alarm. From all sides monks came running, surrounded the gypsies, threw them into a gloomy dungeon and locked the door, posting a guard outside.

Poor Helado and Bota trembled with fear. They knew retribution was at hand, their goose was cooked all right!

"Why so dismal, *chiavalei*?" asked Pichta. "You wait and see. Once morning comes we'll buy our way out. I know all the chiefs here, and I've cash enough, so you've nothing to worry about."

"You've a poor knowledge of the law, *mora*, even though you're a city gent. Why do you think we were scared of entering the church? The only payment for church thieves is your neck. We're done for, all right!"

The brothers mumbled and grumbled, and one told the other, "That's it, brother, you and me, we've done some stealing, enjoyed booty and fame, and now it's over."

At last they fell asleep. Pichta, meanwhile, was only just realizing the danger they were in.

"Oh my God, what on earth brought me to steal? I've enough money to last a lifetime. Now I'm done for."

Such were his gloomy thoughts.

Finally he fell asleep. And as he slept he had a strange

dream: he was lying asleep when a gypsy woman came and shook him by the shoulder.

"Arise, Pichta," she said. "Arise and do as I say."

Up he got.

"In the morning the door will open, the executioner will enter and take you and your fellow thieves to the scaffold. I alone can save you. Think well on it. You have a choice: either you hang or you make me your wife."

It did not take Pichta long to decide. It was surely better to take a new wife than lose a life.

"This is what you must do," the woman continued. "At dawn, as they lead you out, give this envelope to the guard. He will pass it on to his superiors, and it will go ever higher and higher until it reaches the Czar himself.

"But mark my words: all that is written in the envelope will come true. Ask the Czar to free you for two weeks, while the brothers remain locked up till your return. The Czar will agree to your terms and set your free. Then you must go to your wife Ruby and spend three nights with her. But remember: they will be your last three nights together. Go then to the city and await me by the ancient mill."

With those words, the woman vanished as if the ground had swallowed her up. Pichta awoke in a sweat and at once roused the brothers.

"Wake up, lads, wake up, I've just had an amazing dream."

"What sort of dream?" asked the brothers, angry at being disturbed.

"A gypsy woman came and said that if I made her my wife she'd save us. She promised to give me an envelope. I know it all sounds ridiculous . . ."

The brothers stared at Pichta, for in his hand was an envelope with some words inscribed in gold upon it. Exchanging glances, the brothers realized that this had been no dream.

Morning dawned, and all happened as the gypsy woman

said: the cell door opened wide, in came the guards, the envelope was handed over, and the prisoners were locked up once more as the guards went off in haste.

And the strange envelope went higher and higher, up and up, until it reached the Czar himself. And when His Excellency had read the contents, his hands trembled, his gray beard shook with excitement. This is what was written:

The Czar of Russia once had a magic sword, ten generations ago. Wave the sword once and ten men fall down dead; wave it again and a whole regiment expires; wave it thrice and an army is destroyed! The sword served your forbears true and would serve you too, Czar, had it not been lost in years gone by. I alone, Pichta the gypsy, know where to find it. But for that I need your pardon for myself and my companions.

The emperor was much surprised, and not a little doubtful. So he ordered the ancient archives to be dusted off and searched for any news of the wonderful sword. The royal counselors set to poring over the old books. They went back three centuries until they found what they were seeking; there really had been such a magic blade.

When the Czar was informed he called Pichta to him and asked, "Is it true, gypsy, that you can lay your hands on my family's sword?"

"The gospel truth, Your Highness," he said. "Grant me two weeks' grace, and I'll fetch it for you. But on one condition: if I bring you the sword, you must free my two companions and myself."

Of course! The horse-thief brothers and Pichta could have their freedom in exchange for the magic sword.

Mindful of the gypsy woman's word, Pichta set off home to

Ruby, his wife, for three days and nights. How she was overjoyed to see him again, having learned of her husband's fate.

Pichta told all there was to tell, keeping nothing back. And being a wise woman she understood right away.

"You're better off marrying another woman than going to your death," she said. "But don't forget me."

For three nights Pichta remained with his wife and, when his time was up, he gathered his belongings and set off early in the morning for the ancient windmill in the town.

He had to wait awhile before seeing a cloud of dust spiraling to the sky and hearing the thunder of horses' hoofs. As he peered through the dust he saw a carriage pulled by three fine horses, and that same gypsy woman seated in the carriage. Now, Pichta had seen some steeds in his time, the best steeds there were, but he had never set eyes on the like of these. And when he looked upon the gypsy woman in the light of day, his eyes almost popped out of his head, so beautiful was she.

"My name is Zara," she murmured. "Come, sit beside me, dear husband. And even though it is gypsy custom for a wife to obey her man in everything, for two weeks you will do all I tell you."

They traveled through that day and the next, pitching their tent, lighting their fire, as was fitting. On the third morning the gypsy woman said, "Listen, dear husband. I know you are wealthy, a man who's lived a life of ease. But my father is wealthier than you, twentyfold. It is to him we travel now. There we'll spend a week and at its end he'll try to give you anything you ask – fifty horses, a hundred, each pulling a carriage piled high with treasure. But don't take a thing; tell him this: 'Dear father, treasure your daughter like your son. I have no need of your fortune. Just grant me that sword hanging above your bed.' He will be unable to refuse – that is the sword promised to the Czar."

Soon after they arrived at her father's house. Servants came scurrying to help them from the carriage, unhitched the horses, and unloaded their belongings. Then came the master of the house, an old man of some eighty years, with a white beard down to his middle.

"Welcome Zara, my dear daughter. Welcome Pichta, my dear son-in-law. Honor to you, dear guest. Enter my house, I beg of you." Taking Pichta by arm, he led him to a table, and feasting commenced.

Thus the week passed in feasts and merrymaking. No father could have greeted his son-in-law more hospitably. And soon the time came to part. As the old man led out his daughter and her husband, he said, "Servants, harness as many horses as Pichta wishes, and load the carts with treasure."

Recalling Zara's words, Pichta at once said, "See here, dear father, I have no need of your horses or treasure, so much do I have at home. Give me rather the sword that hangs upon your wall."

The old man frowned, stared hard at his daughter, yet had to comply.

"So be it," he said at last. "I'll give you the sword for my daughter's sake."

Off rode Pichta and Zara once more for Moscow, to that selfsame windmill where they had but recently met.

"And now, dear Pichta," she said, "we must part. I shall pitch my tent here and await your return. Meanwhile you go straight to the Czar with this sword, reminding him of his oath. That done, go to your wife, spend three nights with her and return to me, this time forever."

So Pichta did. He came before the Czar, who summoned wise men to examine the blade with utmost care. For three days they sat over it, studying the inscriptions, checking them against the ancient manuscripts. Finally all were agreed: Yes, this was the magic sword. How delighted was the Czar.

"I'll keep my word, gypsy," he said. "I grant freedom to you and your companions. Go where you will, but tell those horse thieves not to steal again or I'll use my sword upon them!"

On the royal pardon, Bota and Helado went free, leapt upon their steeds and could not be seen for dust. To this day I have not seen hair nor hide of either.

Then off went Pichta to his former wife, scarcely dragging his feet towards the house, so much in love with Zara now was he. But he had to keep his word. The three nights passed in some discomfort, and then off he rushed to the old windmill, to the tent where Zara was awaiting him.

"I've done all you said, my darling wife," he said. "What are we to do now?"

"Now, dear husband, we shall live by gypsy custom; you are now master, decide our fate. If you give the word, we'll take to the road. If not, we'll build a mansion. Live as you wish, only never leave me."

Throughout his life Pichta had settled in one place, yet now he wished to roam and see the world.

"Let's go where gypsies will not know us," he said. "After all, what would folk say? That I abandoned one wife and took another? That I had never robbed, yet broke the habit? Let us depart for the south, a thousand miles from here."

It was agreed. They hitched up the horses and set off for distant parts where no one knew them. Along the way they stayed at many gypsy encampments. How the gypsies envied Pichta his lovely wife – no one had ever seen such beauty. And they marveled at the sturdy steeds harnessed to the wagon; each thought to himself what a grand thief the stranger was, what steeds he must have stolen.

Yet as time went on, gypsies came to realize that Pichta really did live by brain and skill. He did not steal, he traded horses. One deal struck, then another, that's the way his wealth increased. So everywhere gypsies welcomed him, and his reputation grew. He was a good man, and poor folk always found comfort from him.

One year passed. Pichta's wife was now with child and gave birth to a son. Zara called her husband to her.

"I know you wish to have our son baptized right away; but pray forgive me, dear husband, I am too weak to go to church. Let us name the boy ourselves. When I am well we can baptize him properly."

"But what name shall we give him?" asked Pichta, agreeing to his wife's request.

Whatever name he suggested, Zara opposed it. He picked his way through a hundred gypsy names, and still none pleased his wife. At last, he said kindly, "Then you give the boy a name, my dear."

"Let's call our son Beng," she said.

"Beng? So be it. Better Beng than no name at all."

That same evening Zara screamed in pain and, calling her husband to her, told him, "Listen closely. You see my pain and torment. You must not come to me for three whole days and nights. Let me be and don't cast a single glance in my direction."

Pichta gave his word, though he was much worried by his wife's condition. Leaving his wife alone in the tent, he went to lie down beneath the wagon. That night and the following day went by without event, yet Pichta was restless.

"I wonder how my poor wife is? Perhaps she needs my help? Perhaps I can fetch her something?"

He so wished to be with her; only his promise held him back. A second night and day passed by, and he was even more worried than before. Just one small peep to see how she was? But he recalled his vow.

The third night came, and his impatience got the better of him.

60

"What a fine to-do!" he cried. "That a man cannot even look upon his own wife!"

And he went straight to her.

On opening the tent flap, he stood rooted to the spot, staring at the scene before him.

Zara was bending over a bowl of water, murmuring some strange words; her eyes shone like glowing coals and her head had sprouted horns. So stunned was he that he let out a wild shriek.

"What have you done?" Zara cried. "Why did you not keep your word? Had you waited till morning, we would have lived together in happiness for the rest of our lives. Now I cannot wash away the devil's curse. Beng shall remain with you, but I must leave you forever. See you look after our son well. In time he will become a famous gypsy to whom gypsies will compose many songs."

Even if Zara had had twenty horns upon her head Pichta would not have left her. He fell upon his knees before her, begging, "My dearest wife, don't go. I do not fear the devil's curse; the horns on your lovely head do not frighten me. Let us continue living as before."

"No, Pichta, we cannot escape our fate."

Zara left the tent and went into the forest, with Pichta trailing behind, crying after her, "Please don't leave me, Zara. Stay!"

The forest grew ever darker and denser. Suddenly Zara halted and turned.

"Hear my final word, Pichta. Return to your tent, take our son and go back to your former wife. Bring up Beng together."

Thereupon she vanished into thin air. All night Pichta rushed about the forest, shouting, calling his wife. Yet only the echo of his voice rang back from the towering trees. Next morning, he retraced his steps to the tent, heartbroken and weary. He harnessed the horses, loaded all his belongings on to the wagon and started off for his old home with Beng.

Ruby was overjoyed to see him. And since she had no children of her own, she took to Beng at once and treated him as her own dear son.

There was just one thing. She did not take too kindly to the name Beng – for that means "devil" in gypsy tongue. So she took him forthwith to church and christened him Vaida, meaning "chieftain." And many are the stories about that wild and handsome gypsy.

NIVASI AND KESALI

It was long ago. A certain gypsy had three daughters with whom he was very strict and stern, not letting them beyond the family tent. So they never saw any other man but their father, nor heard the gossip of the camp. When the time came for them to wed, many were the wealthy gypsies who came to call; yet all left disappointed.

One night, when the sisters were asleep, a little old man appeared in their dreams.

"Come to a clearing in the forest," he said, "and there you'll find an aged oak beneath which an old witch awaits you. She will tell each of you about your destiny, what sort of man you are to wed."

When the sisters awoke, they each told the story of the night just past and decided to go to the clearing to learn about their fate. They found it without difficulty, and there stood the aged oak so huge its crown reached to the sky; beneath its branches sat an old, old crone.

"Let the eldest sister approach," she called.

Timidly, the eldest sister stepped forward.

"Tell me, Grannie," she said, "what is my destiny?"

"It is your fate, my dear, to spend your days inside a cave; you are to be the wife of the cave spirit. He is very rich, there are none richer on earth. Only you will not see daylight again. Prepare yourself for that fate."

"What of my sisters?" asked the eldest sister.

"Forget them, my dear, you'll see them no more."

"I won't marry the cave spirit," the girl exclaimed. "I won't bid farewell to my sisters and the light of day."

"As you will, only beware. The cave spirit will not forgive you; he'll find and punish you."

Next the middle sister was summoned.

"Tell me, Grannie, what is my fate?"

"It is your lot, my dear, to wed the forest spirit. There is none stronger in the world than the forest spirit; he'll shield you from human gaze and tell you tales of forest life. The birds of the air and beasts of the forest will be your only companions."

"What about my sisters?" she asked.

"Cast them from your mind, girl. That is your fate."

"That will not be," the middle sister cried. "I refuse to marry the forest spirit."

"You'll not cheat fate, girl. Watch out for the forest spirit, he'll punish you for those hasty words."

Finally, the youngest sister approached the old crone.

"And what is my fate, Grannie? Tell me the truth, hold nothing back."

"You must go to the lake, sit upon the bank and wait; the waves will part and on to land will step the water spirit with his twelve sons. It is your lot to live with that water spirit within his home. All the wealth of the lake will be yours, though you'll see your sisters no more."

With a sigh, the youngest sister said, "What will be will be. You cannot run away from fate."

As the two elder sisters bade farewell to the youngest, they each went their separate ways: the two eldest girls back to their home, and the youngest off to the distant lake.

As the little gypsy girl arrived at the lakeside, she sat down upon some pebbles and waited. Precisely at midnight the waves parted and out stepped the water spirit, all white and glistening with foam.

"So you've come, daughter?"

"I'm here, Sire."

"You are right not to cheat fate," he said. "Your wish will be mine to command. Do not worry: you'll be my daughter, not my wife. You see, I have a dozen sons, and not one daughter. So we'll look after you well."

The waves parted once more and welcomed the gypsy girl along with the returning water spirit and his sons.

And she lived one year with the water spirit, then a second. The old man could not do enough for her, all but carried her in his arms. As for her new brothers, they loved her with all their heart. It was a happy life in the watery realm, yet just one sadness clouded her joy: she so wished to see her sisters again. And one day she told the water spirit of her desire.

"Do you recall, Sire, promising me a wish, yours to command, you said?"

"Speak, dear daughter, anything you desire."

"I wish to see my sisters again."

The water spirit frowned, his heart was heavy.

"I fear it will not bring you joy," he said.

But the gypsy girl persisted. "Let me go, Sire; whatever the truth may be, it is the truth and cannot be changed."

Thereupon the water spirit waved his hand and gave an order, "My sons, take your sister to her old camp, let her gaze upon the way her sisters now live."

The brothers took their sister by the arms and bore her to the edge of her camp. She went on alone, but soon halted in surprise. Over by some tents two women were calling to young gypsy lads, who were clearly too nervous to approach. The women were as naked as the day they were born, their long tresses reached to their knees, and they were so lovely you could not take your eye from them.

65

Finally, the young lads grew bold and came within arms length of the two women; in a flash the women had seized them — and set to tickling them. Tickled and tickled and tickled them to death.

The youngest sister recognized the two women; and she wept. As soon as they saw her, they came running over, crying, "Forgive us, sister, we did not listen to the crone. This now is our punishment."

"The cave spirit turned me into a *nivasi*, a mermaid, for not marrying him," said the eldest.

"The forest spirit turned me into a *kesali*, a forest spirit for refusing him," said the middle sister. "And neither of us have had peace since. It is our fate to trap unwary youths."

The three sisters sorrowed together awhile, then went their separate ways, each to her own fate.

THE GYPSY WHO DID NOT KEEP
HIS WORD

A gypsy once went off horse-stealing, leaving his family behind within the gypsy camp. They waited one day, a second and a third, but there was no sign or news. Now what? In her alarm, the wife roused the whole gypsy band to go in search. They searched here and there without success, finally deciding that he was dead.

In his memory they held a funeral service, his wife poured out her tears and . . . in the passing of time, cast him out of mind. That's life, isn't it?

But this is the strange story of his disappearance.

In the depths of night he pushed on through the forest and emerged into a glade where he spied a steed of stunning beauty. It stood there quietly grazing. Its mane was long, its tail reached to the ground, and white sparks flew from beneath its hoofs. In a single bound it cleared the entire glade.

How the gypsy longed to catch that steed. Yet every time he approached it darted aside and neighed so hard it made the ground shake. Finally, it galloped off, leaving the gypsy standing and staring. And not a little ashamed.

"I'm no novice at catching horses," he groaned, "yet that horse escaped me. Just wait; I'll tame it yet."

And he took up the chase. That day went by, another dawned, and at last the hoof marks brought him to the entrance of a rocky cave. Without hesitation, he went inside and followed the tunnel down, down into the bowels of the earth. And he found himself in the underground realm of serpents.

The chief Serpent in that realm was a huge twelve-headed monster who made everyone in his power obey him. As soon as he saw the gypsy he flew at him, hissing in an awesome voice, "How dare you enter my kingdom!"

The gypsy tried not to display his fear. "When gypsies see fine steeds," he said, "they give chase wherever the trail leads. So it is; that's how I came here."

"There is no return for you, gypsy," hissed the Serpent. "Now you must make your choice: be my slave or die."

Well, who chooses death?

So the gypsy began to work for the Serpent and was made to groom the enchanted steeds. That suited him well.

One year passed, another and a third. And the busy gypsy earned the admiration of the Serpent, so well did he tend the magic steeds. And one day the Serpent summoned him and said, "What do you say to going home?"

For three whole years the gypsy had thought of nothing else but gazing on his wife and children again. The Serpent's words cheered him no end.

"I'll let you go, gypsy, since you've served me well. But there's one condition: no one must learn of where you have been. If you break that vow your fate is sealed."

Striking the ground with its tail, the Serpent gave a whistle and all the other serpents formed a ball about the gypsy; as the earth opened up the ball of tangled snakes began to roll, with the gypsy caught up inside it. It rolled and rolled until it reached the daylight.

"Climb out," ordered the twelve-headed Serpent.

And the gypsy crawled out into the light of day, stared about him blinking, and did not even notice the ball of snakes disappearing into the ground.

"Mind you keep your vow," hissed the Serpent King.

"On the lives of my wife and children, I shall not tell!" he swore.

And off he ran home. When he appeared, of course, the gypsies thought it must be a ghost. Had he returned from the dead? But he convinced them he was alive and well, and naturally his wife and children were overjoyed.

"Where have you been, dear husband?" his wife asked once they were inside their tent. "How did you disappear for so long? Do tell us."

He was so happy to be back with his family that a mist seemed to cloud his mind, and he forgot his vow. His wife and children listened open-mouthed as he told the story of his adventures underground. Only at the end did he realize what he had done . . .

"Oh, *Devaley*!" he cried. "God, what have I done?"

With a strangled cry, he fell to the ground and began to twist and turn in torment. He twisted, squirmed, writhed . . . and turned into a venomous snake. Then, setting upon his wife and children, he bit each one in turn and his poison struck them down: they fell beside him on the ground, writhing in pain.

Next morning when the gypsies glanced into the tent they saw the wife and children lying cold and dead. And across their lifeless bodies crawled a hissing snake.

DEATH AND THE GYPSY

There was once a gypsy in the world who lived a long life, journeyed down life's highways, and had bright memories of all he'd seen. And with the passing of the years the time came for him to go.

But who wants to die? He was a happy soul, loved to dance, sing and tell tall stories.

Late one night old Dame Death came to him and said, "Right, gypsy, your time's up. That's it. Come along."

"Hold on, old girl," he begged. "Give me an hour or so to say farewell."

"Whatever next! You've had a good life, as it is. Haven't you drunk wine enough? Had your fill of love? Pinched some fine horses in your time? Make ready. We must be off by first light."

"Hold your horses, old girl; the night is still young. Spare me a moment to strum my guitar for the last time, sing a song for my soul."

"Oh, go on then," said Death. "Strum your guitar if it makes you feel better before meeting death."

Picking up his guitar, the gypsy began to play and sing a song. Death just sat there waiting, her mouth wide open. She had never heard such singing before. And she was quite partial to a song. Barely had he finished singing than she was pleading. "Dear fellow, sing another song for me."

"Tickled your fancy, did it?" he said, flashing her a smile and strumming fiercely again.

Then he struck up another tune and began to dance.

"Sing! Sing! Sing!" shouted Death.

The gypsy sang a third song, then a fourth . . .

In no time at all it seemed dawn had crept up on them.

Death had not even noticed night passing. And when the gypsy glanced up old Dame Death was nowhere to be seen.

Next night it began again: once more Dame Death came to the gypsy, and he bewitched her with his singing till dawn.

And so on every night.

That was how the gypsy cheated death.

SARINA

A gypsy chief's wife died. What was he to do? He had a heap
of children to feed and no one to help him. So he thought to
take a new wife.

There was in the tribe a young and beautiful gypsy girl,
Sarina. Many was the lad who had wooed her, yet she had
spurned them all. And now the old chief picked on her; when
Sarina heard of his intentions she turned paler than death and
begged her parents not to force her to wed him.

But how could her parents refuse the chief? There was no
escape: if they left the camp they would surely perish on their
own. So they really had no choice but to give up their
daughter.

Sarina moved to the chief's tent, living as his wife, yet not a
wife at all. It was not long before talk went round the camp
and gypsies cast sly glances at their chief. That angered him,
and he made up his mind to take Sarina by force.

That night he entered his tent and made straight for her.
With a scream she shrank back, hands crossed over her chest.

"Stop!" she cried. "Come no closer."

The chief paid no heed; he came on and seized her. Yet the
moment he touched his young wife he had a dreadful shock:
for his fingers touched a cold, hard form. As he started back in
alarm, he stood and stared . . .

Sarina had turned to stone.

THUNDER CLAP

There was once a handsome, sturdy fellow known as Thunder Clap (don't ask me where he got his name, I don't know). As soon as he came of age, he went out into the world to seek a wife. He was mighty long about his search, looked in many towns and villages, met a host of gypsies – but found none to take his fancy.

Now here he was, wandering along the road, down in the dumps . . . And he came upon an aged gypsy, a tough little fellow, grizzled and wrinkled, with a beard down to his middle.

"Where are you going, lad?" he asked.

"I don't rightly know myself," answered Thunder Clap. "I've been to-ing and fro-ing about the world seeking a wife. Had no luck though – can't find a good match anywhere."

"Now listen here," said the old fellow. "Take that track over there into the forest and you'll come to a cottage; go up to it and you'll hear my daughter's voice calling for help: 'Thunder Clap, save me!' Tell her this: 'I'll save you, but how long before I can free you?' And she will surely say, 'One year or two . . .' That way you'll find a wife."

Thunder Clap thanked the old man and went on his way. On and on he went, came to the forest and, much to his surprise, there was the cottage. But it had no windows or a door, not even a porch. From inside, however, he heard a woman's cry: "Thunder Clap, save me!"

Putting his mouth against the wall, he shouted back, "I'll save you, only how long before I can free you?"

"The time is nigh," the voice called back. "Save me, I'm yours. Go to the wall on the right and knock hard."

In short, he went up to the wall on the right and knocked hard: once, twice – and down fell the wall to reveal a maiden standing there. The moment he set eyes on her he almost lost his mind, so ugly was she!

"Wait, don't run away," said she. "Within three days you won't recognize me, I'll be so pretty."

But Thunder Clap did not stay to find out; covering his eyes, he took to his heels and dashed madly through the forest. He ran and ran and finally came upon the old man once more.

"Why did you not help my daughter?" were the man's first words. "So be it, I'll give you a second chance. Take that road over there and seek your fortune along it."

Thunder Clap did as the old man said, walked on and on until he spied a slender rowan tree; and as he approached, the rowan bent towards him, whispering, "Take my berries and taste them."

"I don't want your berries," he said. "I'm bitter enough without them."

On he went until he came to a crab-apple tree. And that tree bent its branches towards him, murmuring, "Pick my apples, Thunder Clap, taste them."

"I don't want your apples," he said, "my spirit is sour enough without them."

As he spoke those words, the little old fellow sprang from behind the tree, crying, "Thrice I tested you, and thrice you spurned my daughter. I am the forest wizard and I shall punish you."

Waving a switch, he turned Thunder Clap into a little

demon: black hair grew upon his arms, horns sprouted from his head, and a long tail behind. Tossing him up to the tree-tops, the old man sent him bouncing from fir to asp, pine to birch.

How long he was a demon I cannot say; what I know is that the forest wizard's daughter could not shut him out of her mind, and she kept on at her father, "Return him to me, give him one more chance."

Finally the old man agreed. As soon as it was dark and fires lit up the forest wizard's camp, the gypsies saw a black hairy demon in a fir top, waving his arms and shouting, "Let me down, let me down, I'm tired of leaping through the trees."

"Only our elder has the power for that," the gypsy women cried.

"Tell my fortune then," he cried in desperation. "What have I done to deserve this torment?"

Gathering round the fir tree, the gypsy women began to tell his fortune. One called up, "Ekh, dear boy, you suffer for your sins. Good fortune smiled on you thrice, and you turned it down, tossed it away. The first one scared you, the second was too bitter, the third sour. That's why our elder has punished you."

Now he knew. And happy in the truth, cried out, "Thank you, gypsy women, let me show my gratitude. Take my money, all my gold, I give it willingly." And he began to rain gold coins down upon the gypsies – though, in truth, it was autumn leaves.

At that moment the forest wizard left his tent.

"Hey, Grandpa!" cried Thunder Clap. "Take me to that rowan tree, I'd love to taste its berries."

"Very well," the wizard said, flying up to the fir top.

He took the lad by his shoulders and they flew through the forest: in no time they were at the rowan. At once Thunder Clap picked a berry and ate it. So bitter was it, that berry, that

any other time he would have spat it out straightaway, but now he did not even mark the taste. And once he had eaten it, the rowan became a crab-apple tree. Right away he picked an apple and ate it; so sour was it he would have spat it out any other time, but not now. He did not even mark the taste. And the moment he ate the apple, the tree turned into the gypsy maid – so ugly you'd have had forty fits just to see her.

He approached the girl and took her hand, saying gently, "Dear beauty, pray be my wife."

The moment those words passed his lips, the forest wizard waved a switch and the ugly girl turned into a maid more lovely than words can relate or tales can unfold.

Giving the loving pair his blessing, the wizard said, "Live long and be happy."

And so, indeed, they did.

WHY GYPSIES LOVE GOD

It is said that when Jesus was on the cross, a gypsy stood beside him. And someone noticed that they had forgotten to hammer a nail into one of Christ's hands.

"Go on, gypsy," a soldier cried, "knock the nail into his hand."

So the gypsy approached the cross, swung his hammer and then stepped back.

"Well, gypsy, have you done the job?"

"Take a look for yourself," he said. "You can see the blood."

The cross was lifted up, and both hands clearly showed a stain of blood.

But the gypsy had not nailed Christ's hand to the cross; he had squashed a fly that had settled on Christ's palm. And now the fly's blood made it look like that of Jesus — and the fly's remains showed upon the palm like a nail's head.

Since that time Christ has allowed all gypsies to swear by His name. Whenever they are caught stealing, for instance, you'll hear a gypsy say, "As God's my witness, I never stole a thing! Nail me to the cross, for Christ's sake, if I ever cheated you!"

The gypsies know Christ will help them out, just as they helped Him out all those years ago.

THE DEAD ENCAMPMENT

There was once a young horse-dealer from a wealthy clan. One time he went to a horse fair, made a tidy sum, and was on his way home when night overtook him. As he was looking for a spot to pitch his tent he suddenly caught the sound of gypsy singing close by; the voices filled the air like night-time dew. Heading for the sound he soon spied a gypsy camp in a clearing by a river.

Fires blazed all around and gypsies were sitting there singing songs. And what songs they sang! Enough to set you dancing and bring tears to the eye.

He tied his horse to some trees within the wood, and stood watching the scene. Who were these gypsies? Of what tribe?

Curiosity drew him closer and closer to the encampment; but suddenly he stopped, catching his breath, as he saw a beautiful gypsy girl lit up in the fire's glow. So well did she sing and dance that his heart flared up like a bright red flame. And right there he swore he would one day make her his. And when a gypsy makes a vow he has to keep it!

All night long the gypsies danced and sang, yet something made the young gypsy hang back; he did not join them. Just as it grew light he saw the band disperse among the tents, all the while keeping his eyes on the beautiful gypsy girl.

While all was still, he made towards her tent, intending to steal her away as the others slept. Creeping up to the tent, he opened the flap and . . . what a sight met his eyes!

On the ground lay row upon row of gypsies: some with no arms, some no legs, others no heads. It was a camp of dead gypsies! For a while he stood rooted to the spot, but as his fear subsided he set to seeking out the lovely gypsy maid. And there at last she was – sprawled upon the ground, no sign of life, her head, arms and legs lying apart beside her.

Well, a vow's a vow.

"Dead or alive, she shall be mine!" he breathed. "Even if she does only come alive at night . . ."

So he put her pieces into his wagon and drove off with them. All the day he traveled, distancing himself from the dead encampment and, as night descended, the gypsy girl came to life.

"Where are you taking me?" she cried. "My brothers will pursue and kill you; don't you know you cannot hide from the dead? Turn back at once."

"Your brothers do not scare me," said he. "I love you, you shall be mine, dead or alive."

Hardly had he uttered those words than he heard the pounding of horse hoofs: it was the brothers in pursuit. The poor lad was caught and thrashed within an inch of his life, while the sister was carried back to the dead encampment.

It was morning when the gypsy regained his senses; he washed his wounds in a nearby stream and ruminated on his fate: "No, I swore I'd make her mine, I must keep my vow."

Again he set out in search of the dead band of gypsies and once more, as soon as the gypsies retired at dawn, he snatched up the pieces of his beloved and rode off swiftly. As soon as night descended, however, events took the same turn: her brothers took up the chase, beat him black and blue, and took back their sister.

"No, you won't shake me off so easily," the gypsy resolved. "Next time I won't take my wagon; I'll make better time."

So a third time he carried off the gypsy girl, putting the pieces of her body in a sack and flinging it across his horse.

Had his horse matched those of the gypsy brothers he would have escaped; but dead riders have enchanted steeds. While the gypsy had to pick his way through the forest, the magic steeds flew straight; while he had to swim rivers, the steeds ran upon the water. And just as morning dawned, the brothers caught the fleeing pair, yet this time let him be.

"Our sister is not for you," they said. "A dead woman cannot marry a living man. But since you persist, we'll tell you our story – perhaps you can help us. On our travels we camped in a hayfield, at haymaking time. And in the morning peasants set upon us with pitchforks, axes and sickles – all because our horses had spoiled their hayricks. They cut us down, each and every one, and just left us where we lay. That is why our souls now have no rest. If you fetch a priest to bury us properly we will do you no more harm."

He promised to do as the brothers asked, though he did not keep his word completely: the whole camp was buried, as was fitting, all except the lovely gypsy maid – she remained in his wagon.

When she came to life that night, she was very angry.

"What have you done? You did not keep your word to my brothers, so now my soul can never rest and I must roam the earth forever."

So saying, she faded clean away.

As for the young gypsy he lived just three days longer, dying then of a broken heart.

ADVENTURES OF THE GYPSY FOOL

In a certain realm, a certain land, there appeared a Dragon, and no one could find a way past it. First it gobbled a cow, then a sheep, and plenty else besides. In short, misery and woe.

About that time a raggle-taggle gypsy was passing through the realm, as poor as a gypsy tinker ever was. As for his horse, it was a wonder how the bag of bones staggered along. Yet it did, hauling a rickety old wagon full of gypsy wares and a topsy-turvy bunch of barefoot, hungry kids. And to tell you true that gypsy was as stupid as they come, and a scruffy, snotty-nose flea-bag too.

When he reached the forest he called a halt. And what did he do? He set to making a fire, of course. As luck would have it, a pile of brushwood stood piled up in a glade.

So he lit the heap of brushwood from all sides and the blaze as soon spiraled high towards the heavens.

But this was no simple pile of wood; it was the nest of the fearsome Dragon. And now the Dragon burned and squirmed in torment in the gypsy's camp-fire. Its skin cracked so loudly it was like balls fired from a cannon. It woke the Czar in his palace.

"What's going on?" he asked his servants. "What's all that row?"

The monarch was quickly brought a spyglass, and when he peered through it he saw that in the forest where the Dragon lived a fire was blazing; the crackling came from there.

Harnessing a pair of steeds, he rode off to investigate this odd affair; and when he arrived he saw the raggle-taggle gypsy sitting, staring at the burning Dragon. The Czar was much amazed.

"You must be a bold knight, come to slay the Dragon," said the Czar.

"Huh?" said the gypsy rudely.

"I said you must be a knight, you've slain the Dragon."

"Slain the Dragon? So what?" snorted the gypsy.

"Listen, *mora*," said the Czar. "Leave your wife and tent and come to serve me. Think on it, if I take a liking to you, I might even wed you to my daughter, and you'll be rich."

Who would pass up such an offer? It did not take the gypsy long. Fair enough, he'd follow the Czar to the palace.

Back at the palace, the Czar told the gypsy, "My neighbor Czar is a pest; he gives me no peace, and I want to teach him a lesson. I'll give you a thousand men or more to march against him."

"Keep your soldiers," the gypsy said. "I'll do for pests myself. Just give me a witness to prove I'm not cheating you."

Off went the gypsy with a witness to the neighboring realm. Coming to the royal city he lit a fire by the city wall and set to drying his pants – driving out the fleas. Meanwhile he rummaged in his knapsack for a lump of pork, stuck it on a stick and was just about to roast it on the fire when, from out of nowhere, leapt his old dog. It snatched up the meat and, helter-skelter, ran into the city.

That made him lose his temper. "Well I'll be damned! If I let that cur pinch my meat I'll die of hunger."

Snatching up a cudgel, he rushed after the dog for all he was worth. While he was running along, swinging his cudgel, he flattened every soldier in the royal army. All the town's folk fled before him, thinking it was some devil or demon, filthy dirty, no pants on, as black as pitch, and waving a club about . . .

The gypsy pursued the dog right into the palace, knocking everyone out, laying about him to right and left, hurry-scurry, and – biff! – down went the Czar as well.

He got his meat back in the end.

Meanwhile, the witness who was running behind noted down the adventures in every detail.

When the hero gypsy returned to the first Czar, he was naturally received in triumph, with much pomp and awe.

"Sire, pray do us the honor of marrying the princess," begged the Czar. "And stay at our palace as long as you wish."

So a rich wedding banquet was held, and the gypsy took up with the royal princess. But to tell you straight, it didn't suit him at all.

"What sort of life is this?" he thought. "At least my old gypsy wife smelt of firesmoke; God knows what this one smells of, what with all that scent and rouge."

He soon was fed up being wed to the princess. He never stepped foot inside her bedroom, bedded himself down in the stable, and if the princess came to him he had to turn his nose away.

It was not long before the princess was off to her father to complain. "That gypsy doesn't kiss or caress me," she moaned. "And he turns his nose away when I come close. What am I to do?"

"Never mind, dear daughter," said the Czar, "he'll get used to you, just be more tender to him. These rough lads are mighty partial to a wife's caress."

Several days passed. By now the gypsy was at the end of his tether. Going out on to the palace balcony one morning early he saw a village lad passing by. Beckoning him over, the gypsy hopped down and told him plain, "Say, man, I've got myself hitched to the Czar's lass, so on and so forth . . . I'm at my wit's end. It's time for me to hop it back to my old missus."

And he told the lad his plan. The fellow was not against the deal. Would you be? In short, they swapped clothes, the lad putting on the gypsy's glad rags, the gypsy donning the fellow's smock before making tracks for home.

From then on the Czar's daughter was delighted with her husband. "That gypsy's a changed man," she told her father. "He's become so gentle and loving; he even looks different, all white and clean, no longer black and snotty-nosed. He says he washed in three pools of dew and that turned him white."

"There you are," said the Czar with a knowing wink. "I told you it would turn out all right."

In the meantime the raggle-taggle gypsy was back in his own tent, laying about his gypsy wife. "What did you leave me in the lurch for," he cried, "you good-for-nothing hussy? Why didn't you come looking for me?"

Despite the blows, she was glad to see him back, and the kidlings danced about him in delight. And it was not long before they were on the road again, the gypsy way. As for his adventures with the Czar and Dragon, he gave them no further thought.

THREE NINCOMPOOPS

There was once an old gypsy woman with an only son. And the time came for the lad to do his army service. He had his head shaved and was marched off. A year went by, and then another.

One day an unknown gypsy entered the camp dressed in soldier's uniform. Coming up to the old gypsy woman, he said, "Hello there, Grandma, your son sent me. We're soldiering together, and I'm home on leave. He sends his best regards and asks a favor."

The gypsy woman beamed. "Ai, thanks for the news, sonny. Tell me what he wants, I'll do all he says."

"It's a tough life," said the soldier. "The food's dreadful, they clothe us badly. Just look at the state I'm in."

Sure enough, the old lady could see his uniform was full of holes.

"Your son asks for as much food as you can spare, any old clothes and boots . . ."

Into the tent went the gypsy woman, grubbed about and came out with all she had, tied in a bundle, and handed it over to the stranger.

"Take it, laddie, give it to my son with all my love."

Off went the gypsy, even before the woman had time to ask his name.

Time went by and the son returned. How glad his mother was to see him.

"Oi, my lad, back home at last. How I've waited for you, thought of you every day. A good job your comrade brought me news; I hope you liked the food and clothes I sent."

"What comrade?"

"I don't know his name," she said. "I didn't ask."

"Oh, Mother, how stupid of you," said her son angrily. "How could you give things to the first man who comes along? I won't stay here any longer. But if I find a person more stupid than you I'll forgive you and return."

Off went the gypsy on his travels, wondering whether he would find anyone more stupid than his mother. Whether he journeyed far or near I did not hear, but finally he came to a wealthy farm. And there, right in front of the house was a sow with piglets. Taking off his hat, the gypsy knelt down in the mud and began to bow before the sow. Just then the lady of the house emerged, took one look at the gypsy and cried in amazement, "What are you doing groveling before our sow?"

"Dear lady," the gypsy called back, "it's our hog's wedding day; I'm here to invite pigs from all around to the wedding."

With that he bowed once more to the pigs, muttering, "Dear sow, don't refuse, do come to the wedding . . ."

"Stop bowing and scraping in the mud," the mistress said. "It really isn't worth getting on your knees for; just pick her up along with the piglets, and be done with it."

So the gypsy gathered up the sow and piglets, thrust them into a sack, and addressed the lady once more, "What can I take them to the wedding in?"

"How foolish your are," she replied. "Take my carriage and travel there in style."

Thereupon the gypsy hitched up the horses, loaded the sow and piglets into the carriage, and went on his way. As he was on the road, he thought to himself, "It seems there are folk

88

even more foolish than mother . . ."

Along the road he spotted a squire galloping towards him on a handsome mare. Springing down from the carriage, the gypsy snatched off his hat and swiftly placed it over a tree stump at the wayside. As the squire rode up he asked, "What's up, gypsy?"

"See here," came the reply, "I've caught a firebird. If only I can get home quickly I'll fetch my book of magic and put a spell on it. That's the only way to trap a firebird."

"Let me keep watch, gypsy," said the squire. "You go for the magic book."

"Oh, squire, my horse's too slow; I fear the firebird will escape before I return."

"Then take my mare," cried the squire, beaming widely. "Hitch her to the carriage and go like the wind. I'll sit here waiting."

So the gypsy hitched on the mare, turned the carriage about and rushed off at full speed. Meanwhile the squire sat there beside the hat, awaiting the gypsy's return . . . It was several hours later that he began to have his doubts. Cautiously, he lifted the hat and stared down at the stump. Spitting with rage, he set off home on foot.

The gypsy rode back home in style, showing off his carriage pulled by the handsome pair of steeds, and the sow and piglets into the bargain. As his mother ran out to greet him, he called to her, "Well now, mother, I traveled about the world and found folk who are bigger nincompoops than you are. I gladly forgive you and will never roam again."

THE GYPSY AND THE WOLF

A pack of wolves was led by a sly old beast who had seen many dangers in his long life. He had spat in death's eye many a time, yet emerged triumphant from all his fights.

That old wolf knew the forest laws, knew the forest did not spare the weak, knew also that one day he would be too old to lead the pack. Then they would not spare him.

Though his old wounds prevented him from hunting as well as in his younger days, he still got by with cunning, and always ran on ahead to seek out the prey.

But one cold winter the hunting was lean; and for the first time he saw hatred and contempt in the pack's gray eyes. No longer were young wolves afraid of him; they knew he was getting old. The entire pack had patiently awaited this moment when it could turn on its once-strong leader.

It was then he made up his mind.

Waiting till deepest night, the old wolf rose silently and started to slink away, distancing himself from the hungry wolves. But they sensed his flight and took up pursuit, though they were not as wise in forest lore as he. He kept just ahead of them, making for a clearing where he knew a lone gypsy's cottage stood.

At one time that gypsy, too, had been leader of a pack. And what a mighty gypsy pack it was! He had led his gypsies down many tracks, had been wise and bold; his word had often saved the pack from misfortune.

The time came, however, when old age withered the leader's strength, he could feel it in his bones: he was not strong enough to hold the reins, to keep young braves in check.

One time, when the clan was wintering in a village and the gypsy families were quartered in huts, the old chief summoned up his remaining strength and stole away to build himself a cottage in the forest. And that spring, when the gypsy band moved off, the chief was not with them; he remained alone in the forest. No one had seen him, he must have fallen victim to hungry wolves or vanished into a snowdrift.

He did run into wolves, true enough. Yet though he was quite unarmed, the wolf pack did not touch him: their leader had forbidden it. The old man knew not why.

So the gypsy lived alone amidst the towering wood. He feared no one and when one night he heard an eerie wolf cry near his hut, he lit a torch and opened the door. The yellow-flecked gray eyes of the old wolf stared up at him, as if asking for aid. At the margin of the trees, he could see the wolf pack waiting to attack. But as he swung his torch, the wolves slunk back, merging with the gloom.

And the two old-timers, the gypsy and the wolf, looked fondly at each other; the gypsy patted the old leader's furry head as he lay meekly at his feet.

GYPSY PORRIDGE

There was once a poor gypsy who had so many children he could hardly feed them all. Sitting by the fireside, deep in thought one day, he suddenly sees this lord heading for him.

"How can I cheat this dandy?" he thinks.

Now there was porridge cooking on the fire, it was bubbling and burping at that very moment. Quickly the gypsy grabs a bowl of boiling porridge and sets it in the dirt; then he bends over the bowl mumbling mumbo-jumbo. As the lord comes closer he wonders, "What an odd sight. There's a bowl in the dirt, no fire, and the porridge boiling away."

"What's up, gypsy?" he asks.

"What's up?" says the gypsy. "Why, can't you see? I'm cooking porridge."

"What porridge? There's no fire. How can you cook porridge without fire?"

"Like this. You see, my bowl's no ordinary bowl: I give it the gypsy word and the porridge boils all by itself."

"Here, gypsy, sell me that magic bowl, I'll pay you well. How much do you want?"

"It'll cost you dear, lord. And anyway I'm not keen to part with my magic bowl."

"Come now, gypsy, if you know the magic word, you can

make as many bowls as you wish. Sell me your bowl."

"Oh, all right, I'll sell, but this bowl here won't boil by itself. You see this stick I'm stirring the porridge with? Without the stick you won't cook a thing; so you'll need the stick as well."

"Oh very well," said the lord. "Name your price."

"Two hundred rubles, and *Dza devlesa* – God go with you."

The lord counted out the money, took the stick and bowl, and hurried off. Nor did the gypsy linger long; he gathered up his belongings, set his wife and children on the wagon and trundled off in the opposite direction.

Unhappily for him, his litle nag was on its last legs and could hardly pull the wagon. It took an age to reach the nearest village; there the gypsy purchased a brand new horse, swapped his tent, clothed and fed his children, then pushed on farther. When he reached the open plain, he stopped to think, "Now what if that lord catches me? And, as God's my witness, he surely will!"

And talk of the devil! There he was as large as life, riding hard. In an instant the gypsy snatched up a whip and, whispering two words to his wife, swish, swish, swish across her back! But it was all pretense, the whip just skimmed her rump. Yet how she howled, writhing on the ground like some wounded serpent.

When the lord saw the gypsy he shouted out, "Hey, you so-and-so, how dare you trick me!"

Lowering his whip the gypsy gaped at the lord. "How do you mean, tricked you?"

"I set the bowl on the ground, stirred the water with the stick, and all I got was a cold mess!"

"Ah, but did you say the gypsy word?"

"What word?"

"There, you see, you didn't ask about the word, and here you go bawling your head off."

The lord at once calmed down, stroking his chin. "Tell me, gypsy, what is this gypsy word?"

"Just hold on, lord, let me have done with my wife, then we'll talk about it." So saying the gypsy once more laid about his wife.

"Steady on, gypsy, you'll beat her to death."

"Fear not, lord, I've got myself a talk-back wife and so I must teach her to behave. I tan her hide and then, when I crack this whip, she'll jump up as right as rain, ready for orders."

So saying the gypsy cracked his whip and his wife leapt up, as if nothing had happened, hugged her husband and murmured sweetly, "Darling husband, I'll do anything you say."

"Light the fire, cook my tea, feed the children, put them to bed, then sit by the fire and sing till dawn."

"Anything you say, dearest husband," the gypsy wife said before going to fetch firewood.

Meanwhile the lord was thinking to himself, "I could do with a whip like that to teach my wife a lesson; she's got out of hand."

"I say, gypsy, what about selling me that whip?"

"Dare say I could, but it'll cost you dear."

"I'll pay anything, name your price."

"Three hundred, and *Dza devlesa*."

The lord counted out the coins, took the whip and was about to depart when he turned abruptly back.

"Oh no, my lad, you won't trick me again. What's the magic word?"

The gypsy muttered two words into his ear, and off went the lord quite satisfied. Straightaway the gypsy hitched his horse to the wagon and again set off, distancing himself from the lord. This time he bought himself a brace of steeds and a pile of good things for the family.

In the meantime, all the way home the lord repeated the

magic gypsy word. Over and over and over . . . and then forgot.

"Never mind," he mused, "that whip'll teach my wife a lesson without the gypsy word."

As he reached home, he set about his wife at once, brandishing the whip – that'll teach her good and proper! And she, poor woman, howled and wailed.

"Don't you worry, mistress," cried the lord, "I've only got to crack the whip and you'll jump up as good as gold."

Yet by the time he gave the whip a crack, his poor wife had given up the ghost. He seized his head in despair, then strode off in a fury to find that trickster. It took him two long years, but at last he traced the rascal.

Seeing the lord approaching, the gypsy thought his end had come. What could he do?

It was in the midst of winter; the snow was deep, the frost was fierce. Suddenly he had an idea: he dashed inside his tent, stripped naked, snatched up his shirt and rushed outside into the snow. There he leapt up and down, waving his shirt above his head and shouting, "Oi-yoi-yoi, what a heat-wave!"

"Now I've got you, gypsy," yelled the lord. "Your end has come; you won't go cheating honest folk again."

"Hold on, lord, at least give me a chance to cool off before I die. I can't stand this heat. Oh me, Oh my!" All the while he hopped about in the snow like a cat on hot bricks.

"How peculiar!" thought the lord. "It's freezing cold; I'm frozen stiff in this fur coat, yet here's this gypsy jumping about in his birthday suit, fanning himself with his shirt."

"What's the game, gypsy, you can't be hot?" the lord growled suspiciously.

"See here, this shirt's magic. No frost worries me. It's bad enough now, but if I put on this shirt, I'm sweating like a pig."

"Um, listen, gypsy," said the lord, "sell me your shirt."

He was thinking to himself, "Rather than buy expensive

furs and clothes, I'd do better with this magic shirt. It'll be warm and light."

"I suppose I could sell it," he said slowly, "only it would cost you a pretty penny."

"Name your price."

"A thousand rubles, and *Dza devlesa*."

Counting out his money, the lord took the shirt and – set off homeward.

When he arrived home, he summoned all the folk around and began to boast of his new magic: "Just see this, people, it's a magic shirt. It protects me from the cold."

The lord took off his fur coat, removed all his clothes and there he was, as naked as the day he was born, running about the yard waving his shirt in the air.

The good folk gasped in amazement.

"Must be off his rocker, that old lord, Christmas right around the corner, and here he is jumping around in the nude . . ."

Being too ashamed to admit that the gypsy had done him yet again, he carried on his prancing. "Oh, Oh, Oh, how hot I am," he cried, "I can't stand the heat."

He yelled and wailed, brayed and neighed, and . . . was frozen stiff!

As for the gypsy, with the money from the lord he lived with his wife and pile of children happily for the rest of his days.

THE NIGHT BIRD

This happened long ago. A band of gypsies would travel the land and, when they met another tribe, would often come to blows. All because of the chiefs – their word was law. Gypsies were killing each other for nothing, nothing at all. And there arose a hatred among the tribes.

But there was one gypsy who could not bear the strife; he was bent on putting an end to it. So he went to the chief of his tribe and said, "Why do we slay our brothers? Can we not live in peace?"

"Every tribe takes its own road," the chief replied. "Each must go its own way, the tracks should never cross, or trouble starts."

"Why should that be, *Baro Shero?*" asked the young gypsy. But he received no answer.

Whereupon he left the camp and went to other gypsies.

"What clan are you, friend?" he was asked.

"This and that, such and such," said the gypsy about himself. "I want to know how hatred arises between us, why we slay our brothers."

The gypsies made no reply. They hated the other tribe of the evil chief and had lost many lives because of him. All the same, they did not lay hands on the gypsy; they just drove him from their camp.

Many other camps he visited, but nowhere was he listened to, nowhere could he find a resting place.

So he began to live in the forest.

Ever since he was a child he had always been kind and gentle, yet once alone in the forest he grew harsh and bitter and was filled with evil thoughts of revenge against the gypsies. And when he died his spirit became a black night bird; whenever it cried at night someone in a gypsy camp would die.

Meanwhile the band of gypsies of the cruel chieftain continued its journey, and in time it arrived at the dark forest of the night bird, the harbinger of doom.

The gypsies lit their fire unsuspecting, yet were somehow uneasy, as if sensing danger lurking in the trees. No one sang, no one danced. They sat about the fire in silence. All of a sudden, as the fire's embers began to fade, they heard a crying sound above the trees, and a shadow passed above the clearing. That shadow's cry was as heart-rending as a child's in pain.

Everyone trembled. Men tried to fan the flames; they threw on dry twigs to brighten up the gloom. Only the chieftain's little grandson let out a happy cry, "See if I don't catch that night bird and bring it back."

And off he ran boldly into the trees chasing the shadow. Although the other gypsies searched all through the night, the boy was never seen again.

"There's a curse on this place, brothers," shouted the chieftain next morning. "Saddle your horses and let's away."

But next night the cry of the night bird came again, and once more a shadow fell over the camp, this time carrying off the chieftain's son.

In the morning the chieftain sat upon a rock, holding his head in his hands, and he remained like that till sunset. When darkness fell and the night bird raised its voice, the chieftain stood up, crying, "Forgive me, gypsies. It was for me the night bird came, not you."

So saying, he strode off into the forest and was never seen alive again.

Since then the curse on the gypsy tribe disappeared: never again did the night bird's shadow pass above the camp and no more gypsies met a sudden death. Nor did the tribal hatred long remain; soon gypsies began to meet each other as brothers, and peace came to the clans.

HOW A GYPSY WENT IN SEARCH
OF WOE

There were once some gypsies and they had an only son. The family was well off, never short of food, nor knowing need. In the passing of time the son grew to manhood and set to thinking about his life.

"We live well," he told his parents, "we know no hardship, so tell me what is want and woe."

"Better not to know, dear son," they said.

Seeing he would learn nothing from his parents, the lad then asked his grandmother. "Tell me, Grandma, what's want and woe."

"Want and woe," his grandmother said, "that's a tricky business, gypsy business. Now, if you're caught stealing, or fall sick when on the road, or have an empty belly . . . that's want and woe."

Thinking hard, he finally decided, "I'll go into the world and look for want and woe; for sure, I won't find them here. Perhaps I'll try some stealing, as Grandma said."

So off into the world he went. Somewhere on his travels he learned of a fine steed in a merchant's stable.

"If I do steal that horse it means I'm lucky," he thought to himself. "If not I'll know what's woe."

No sooner had he broken the lock of the merchant's stable than the owner appeared gun in hand.

No questions. He shot the gypsy dead.

Picking up the body, the merchant dragged it into the forest and nailed it to a tree.

Let that be a lesson to all gypsies!

Time passed. One day a poor gypsy was traveling through the forest when he halted for the night, pitched his tent, lit a fire, and sat down to drink his tea. Midnight came. All of a sudden, the poor man glanced up and spied a figure walking through the trees, gypsy-like, singing a song:

> I once knew no woe,
> So to seek it I'd go;
> Found it, Oh, Oh . . .
> Woe now I know.

Harkening to the voice and staring hard, the gypsy recognized the figure as the wealthy gypsy's lost son.

"Hey, come and warm yourself," he called.

But the lad would not approach the flames. It's well to know that ghosts do not like fire, though the poor gypsy was not to know that.

Next morning saw the gypsy on the road and approaching the camp of the dead lad's parents.

"Have you seen your son?" he asked.

"No, he's been gone over a month," they said. "He went in search of woe."

"I saw a gypsy in the woods, the dead image of your son," said the other. "I tried to call him, but he would not come."

"Where was that?"

"In such-and-such a place . . . If you don't believe me, I'll take you to the spot."

Off went three men: father, uncle and the poor gypsy. And they came to the selfsame spot where the sight was seen; they lit a fire and sat there waiting. At twelve o'clock a song rang

101

out through the trees:

> I once knew no woe,
> So to seek it I'd go;
> Found it, Oh, Oh . . .
> Woe now I know.

At once the father recognized his son's voice; yet no matter how loud he yelled, how hard he tried to catch the figure, it was no good. At last the truth dawned on him: his son was dead, it was his spirit wandering restlessly in the forest.

"We'll have to wait till morning," the father told the others. "He'll vanish at the third cockcrow, then we must look for the body."

When day broke, the gypsies went off in search: in tree and bush, gully and glade, until finally they found the poor lad nailed to a tree. Taking down the body, they laid it on a cart and took it home.

Father and mother shed bitter tears over their dead son, but made up their minds: he should be remembered. So they built a vault of pure gold and hung his coffin on golden chains within the vault. No funeral service, it was too late for that.

From then on, at nightfall, the dead man would come home and talk to his parents, returning to the vault at the third cockcrow.

One day the father heard tell of a pretty maid in a band of passing gypsies, and thought to marry his son to her. But how? By day the lad lay dead, by night the other gypsies slept. At last, he decided to take his son at night; ribbons were wound into the horses' manes, the green birch pole was stuck with hundred-ruble notes, and gold chains were hung about their necks – all according to gypsy custom.

The gypsies were much surprised at receiving night-time matchmakers.

"What sort of groom is it," they complained, "that comes at night?"

"Our son is very busy, at horse fairs, tending his herd of a hundred steeds, doing deals. In short, his day is full. That's why we have to hold the wedding at night."

The girl took a liking to the young man and gave her consent, so her parents agreed to a night-time wedding.

Once the wedding was over, the young pair began to live together. It was an odd life, sure enough: by day the wife saw nothing of her husband. He would bid farewell to her at dawn, saying he had to go about his affairs, and he would return on the stroke of midnight.

One year passed. And the young man's parents made ready one day to go to market. Before leaving they called the bride to them, saying, "Here are the keys to all the rooms, the barns, the stores and chests – just in case you need something from them. Take what you will, open any door, any lock. But there's one thing: here is a tiny key. On no account open anything with it . . . ."

So saying they departed. The girl was aflame with curiosity. "I wonder why?" she mused. "Why may I open all locks, yet none with this tiny key?"

And she set to searching – what door was it the little key would open? She went round all the barns, tried all the locks, but the key fitted none. Then she ventured abroad, entered the forest and suddenly saw the golden vault with a tiny lock hanging on the door. Boldly she fitted the tiny key into the lock and . . . the door scraped open. In she went and peered through the gloom: a coffin dangled on golden chains from the domed roof, with steps leading upwards.

Climbing up the steps, the gypsy girl looked into the coffin and . . . Oh dear me!

Her husband lay there stone cold dead.

At once she realized why the matchmakers came at night,

why they wed by candle-light, why she saw her husband only after midnight.

Climbing back down the steps, she locked the vault and returned home. When her husband's parents came back she said not a word.

That night, though, when her husband entered, he spoke angrily, "Why did you come to the vault? You had no right. Now you'll be scared of living with me and I'll see you no more."

"I won't leave you," she cried. "I love you dearly and want to help you; perhaps my godfather can help, he's a wise man."

Her husband would hear nothing of it. "Dead bodies should stay dead," he said when she suggested he might be brought to life.

She saw there was no reasoning with him, so she resolved to use her guile. In the morning, when her husband had gone, she ran to her godfather and told him the tale.

"I'll tell you what to do," the godfather said. "As soon as he appears, you must seize and bind him tightly and take him to church, then pray over him for forty days and nights. Only then will he come to life."

She awaited her chance, then one day when her in-laws went off to distant relatives, she called her brothers to help and they carried the coffin into the house.

At midnight, the moment the dead gypsy rose from his coffin bed, they grabbed him, trussed him up, pitched him face downwards in a cart and took him off to church, as the godfather had said.

And the gypsy maid began to pray over her husband's body. All of a sudden, a fearful noise arose inside the church, evil spirits flew about, tormenting the poor girl: they pulled her hair, pinched her arms, scratched her legs, spat in her face and threw dirt and filth all over her. She barely managed to endure it till the third cockcrow, when the demons swept out like a whirlwind.

"I cannot stand it," she told her godfather next morning. "If this is the first night, what will happen next?"

"Fear not, my child," he said, "I'll teach you what to do. Mark a circle about the coffin, let the shadow of a cross fall upon that circle and no evil spirit will enter."

That she did. Next night was easier. No demons could touch her now, no matter how hard they tried: the shadow of the cross within the circle blocked their path.

And she prayed hard, day after day, night after night.

How tired she was, poor girl, yet somehow she kept awake until the final night. But now her eyes would not keep open, so she took a burning candle and thrust her hand into the flame. The pain drove all sleep out of her head, and she managed to pray until the rays of dawn shone through the door.

At the third cockcrow her husband sat up and rubbed his eyes. He was alive and well, thanks to his wife's devotion.

And the happy pair lived long in peace and happiness by day and night.

MARICHKA

This happened in olden times. A gypsy band was wandering about the land led by an old *ataman* who was wise and strong. And great was his hold over the gypsies. All had to obey; swift retribution awaited any waverer.

Now this *ataman* had a beautiful wife and a daughter whose name was Marichka. How the gypsy men envied the chief his strength, wisdom and power, how they envied him his lovely wife – though no one dared to show it.

But there was one gypsy in the band who not only envied him, he had fallen wildly in love with his wife. And so enflamed with passion was he that he vowed nothing would stand in his way. No one knew of this love, he concealed it well; only the *ataman*'s wife noticed his ardent glance, though she kept silent, not wishing to hurt her husband, and perhaps fearing he would punish the reckless gypsy should he know. Why spill blood needlessly?

For a long time the young gypsy kept his feelings to himself, but finally they boiled over and he lay in wait to kill the chief. One morning early, before the sun was up, he hid behind a tree at the edge of the woods, leapt out and plunged a long knife into the leader's heart.

No one would have known of the murder had not Marichka, the dead man's daughter, gone for water at that early hour; she had glanced towards the leafy oak beneath which the deed was done. She told nobody of what she had seen that morning.

From then on the murderer became leader of the clan; he

wielded power over people and, of course, forced the dead chief's widow to become his wife.

As Marichka grew up she became more and more beautiful, as graceful as her mother had once been; and though her heart harbored thoughts of revenge, she always appeared kind and gentle to the new *ataman* – she did not wish him to guess her secret.

She was biding her time.

Yet when she began to feel his glance upon her, she realized the time for revenge was nigh.

One day the *ataman* told Marichka to meet him at dawn within the forest, and she agreed. They met beneath that selfsame leafy oak, on the very spot where her father had been struck down. And now, as the gypsy stretched out his arms to embrace her, a terrible scream rent the still air . . . and steel glinted in his breast.

HOW FEDOT OUTWITTED THE DEVIL

An old gypsy by the name of Fedot lived in a certain gypsy tribe. And what a Rom he was: over six feet tall and hard as nails. Nothing scared him. He'd take on a whole regiment of soldiers if need be. Old Fedot would take up his *shoshka*, swing it round his head and lay out thirty men at once. The only weapon he ever used was his *shoshka*, nothing else.

Our story begins one wintertime.

The gypsy clan wished to seek shelter in a certain village. But, as bad luck would have it, times were hard, and no hut had room for gypsy families. Even Fedot, whom everyone knew, could find no lodgings.

On the very edge of the village, however, dwelt a peasant who had had many dealings with Fedot, and had never once been cheated. And when the peasant learned that Fedot wished to winter thereabouts he shook his head.

"Willingly, I'd let you have my hut, old friend, but woe upon woe: my wife died a while back and comes to haunt me every night. The old dame gives me no peace: no sooner am I bedded down than she's in and out of the place, cussing and fussing; I've had to move in with a neighbor."

"Right, Kuzma," said Fedot. "The dead don't scare me; no ghosts, no devils, no walking dead. Come on, open up and I'll move in with my gypsy clan."

"Well, don't say I didn't warn you," said the old peasant.

So the gypsies took over the hut, made themselves at home, brewed some tea, put the children to bed, and bedded down themselves a little later. Only Fedot remained awake, sitting on the warm stove smoking his pipe and fogging up the room.

The moment midnight came, however, the outside door creaked open and the old dame appeared. It was not the first time she'd set eyes on Fedot, so she now made bold with him. "Aren't you scared of ghosts, Fedot?"

"What's there to be scared of?" he muttered.

In actual fact he was scared out of his wits, but he tried hard not to show it, pulling on his pipe and muttering through his teeth, "Oh no, my beauty, you don't frighten me."

"If you aren't afraid, then why have you brought the whole gypsy tribe in with you?" she jeered.

And she walked among the sleeping gypsies, babbling some sleeping spell to keep them quiet. Then she went over to the cots where the babies slept and started rocking them: she rocked and rocked, rocked and rocked until the poor babies were foaming at the mouth.

That made Fedot's blood boil. "You stop that, old dame, or I'll knock the stuffing out of you."

In a flash she turned and pounced on him, all claws and sharp fangs. What a struggle ensued! The whole hut was turned inside out, the gypsies trampled underfoot – though they did not notice it in their sleep.

Fedot and the old dame went crashing through the door on to the porch, out into the yard, scratching and biting and punching for all they were worth. Despite his great strength, there was nothing Fedot could do to overcome the dead dame.

After a time he was down on his knees, still bravely putting up a fight, though his strength was ebbing fast. Luckily for him the sun rose and saved him from death: as the third cockcrow rang out the old dame vanished as if swallowed up by the earth.

Later that morning Kuzma appeared. "Well now, gypsy," he said, "I did tell you not to stay in the house. But you wouldn't listen. Now you know that what I said is true."

Turning to the other gypsies, he asked, "Didn't you hear anything?"

"We didn't hear or see a thing," they replied. "But our backs ache as if someone's been jumping on us."

All the same, Fedot would not give in.

Next night all happened as before: the old dead dame appeared at midnight, put the gypsies into a deep sleep and set to fighting Fedot. No matter what he hit her with – his *shoshka* or his fists – it had no effect. On and on they tussled till third cockcrow. By then Fedot was at the end of his tether.

Cock-a-doodle-do! In the nick of time.

Sitting wearily on the porch, trying to get his breath, Fedot thought to himself, "One more night like this and I'm a goner; bang down the lid, that ghost'll finish me off. I'll have to find some other way of dealing with her or we'll all be finished."

"Hey, Kuzma," he asked later that day, "where's your missus buried?"

The peasant led him to the graveyard and showed him the grave: it had no cross, nor a fence around it.

"There you are!" exclaimed Fedot. "That's why her soul is restless. Now I know how to deal with her."

And, going into the forest, he cut a solid aspen stake and hammered it into the grave; then he placed a wooden cross at one end, and made a fence about the grave.

And never again did the old dame go a'haunting.

THE BOLD BANOTERY GYPSY

This was long ago. There lived on earth a tribe of Banotery gypsies, some poor and some rich. Wherever their bold chief went the gypsies were sure to follow.

But they fell upon hard times, were down to just a score of families, no more. They had no money, no passports, and now they were wandering deep in the forest to evade military service. In those days soldiering was different from now – they kept you in the army twenty-five years, and that was a lifetime in those days!

Who would freely give up their child to the army? Among gypsies rich or poor, a child is as sacred as a crust of bread.

So here were the Banotery gypsies sheltering in the forest, cold and hungry, feeding on whatever was at hand, catching fish, picking mushrooms, begging bread in woodland hamlets for their children.

Now, in that band of gypsies was a little fellow, no bigger than a child, yet with a broad pair of shoulders and uncommon strength. He would say of himself, "I may be small, but I'm tough and bold. The whole world fears me. Just try me at any deed, I'm ready for anything."

In the passage of time the band came to the land of a certain duke who was full of woe; an ogre had pitched his tent in the duke's forest and would let no one through. If anyone ventured into those parts he would not return.

No matter what the duke did he could not rid himself of the pest. He sent forth peasants with pitchforks and cudgels – but not one returned. He sent in the army, but not a single soldier was seen again. At last he put up a sign at the forest edge:

NO ROAD AHEAD ON FOOT OR HORSE

The Banotery gypsies came one day upon the sign. The chief read out the words and a buzz of excitement went round the band; at once a shrill voice piped up, "Well, *Romaly*, I'm not scared of ogres or wild beasts. I'm going into the forest."

Despite their attempts to stop him, the little gypsy marched off through the trees, a stout stick on his shoulder.

After a while he heard a snorting and roaring – what a dreadful racket! It did not take him long to trace the row; he disappeared into a clearing and there was the ogre lying on the ground snoring away in the sunshine. The ogre's head was like a crocodile's, his tail went three times round the glade, and roaring fire was coming from his nostrils as he snored.

Stout stick in hand, the little gypsy crept up on the sleeping giant, then stopped in his tracks as the ogre stirred, turned over and began snoring again.

Just one mighty blow between the ears – and the ogre departed for the other world! Opening his jaws to make sure he was well and truly dead, the bold little gypsy pulled out a giant fang and marched off back to the waiting gypsy band.

After recounting his tale, he shouted at them, "You are always chattering; one says he's poor, another weak, a third stupid. You gypsies are afraid of your own shadows. Be bold like me. Go forth and fight all ogres, live or die!"

Now it should be said that the duke on whose land the

gypsies had strayed hated gypsies and now gave orders for them to be driven off. He did not yet know of the ogre's fate. Thus, when the duke's men rounded up the gypsies and warned them of the ogre, the bold little gypsy shouted out, "You're too late; that old ogre's dead and gone. I put paid to him myself."

The soldiers burst out laughing.

"You lying vagabond," cried the officer. "A whole platoon of my men marched against him and did not return. How could a squirt like you slay him?"

"If you don't believe me, come and see," said the gypsy, grabbing the officer's arm and dragging him to the clearing in the forest. It was not long before the officer was convinced.

"The duke has ordered," said the officer, "that whoever slays the ogre will be free of army service and, if a vagabond, will be given a passport as well."

"Then take me before the duke at once," cried the bold little gypsy, tightening his grip on the soldier's arm.

So they came before the duke.

"I'm a gypsy. I slew your ogre," announced the little man, showing the ogre's fang.

The duke scowled as he stared at a gypsy he so despised; but he could not go back on his word.

"Show me the deed at once!" he said.

"Just hold on, Duke," said the bold little gypsy. "First give me food and drink, then when I've refreshed myself I'll take you to the forest."

So the gypsy was fed and given drink. He took his ease, then when quite refreshed went off at the head of an entire regiment to show off the slain ogre. However, before they came close to the ogre's glade, the regiment had taken to their heels and fled, the duke in the lead.

"What a babble of babies!" said the gypsy, spitting in disgust. "I'll have to take the ogre to them then."

So he went on, came to the ogre's corpse, took it by the shoulders and dragged it before the duke.

"Do you see this?" he asked the duke.

"I do."

"Is he done for?"

"Done for."

"Right, now keep your promise," the bold little gypsy said. "Free the gypsies from soldiering, give us passports, and don't touch our tribe again or I'll give you a taste of what I gave the ogre!"

Afraid of the bold little man, the duke willingly did all he said. Henceforth the Banotery gypsies could live freely on his estate to their heart's content. As for the bold little gypsy, he was made captain of the duke's army. And who would say he did not deserve it?

THE CHESTNUT BAY

A gypsy once went to market, traded horses with great cunning, made a pot of money, and gained a fine mare into the bargain. Before returning home, he bought himself plenty of food, some fancy clothes, and had a drink or two. Then chirping happily to himself, he set off for home.

"The wife'll be glad, the kids'll be glad,
With bellies filled with jellies."

Night overtook him on the way. So he called a halt, lit a fire, set to roasting meat and brewing tea. And just as he was about to eat, a little old man appeared from the trees and stood before him.

"Hail, fine fellow," the old 'un cried. "What's up here?"

"This," he said, "and that . . . on my way home, did well at market, having a bite to eat."

"Ai-yai! young whipper-snapper," said the old 'un, "take pity on a poor old body; I'm fair famished, worn-out, with holes in my boots, my clothes are rent and worn. Would you give me a sit-down at your fire and a bite to eat?"

The gypsy was pleased to have company.

So the old man tucked in greedily: he ate and ate, gobbled and chewed, wailing all the while, "Begrudge me naught."

And he finished off all the food the gypsy had bought at market. Wiping his whiskers, the old boy said at last, "Hey, gypsy lad, can you put a stitch of clothing upon my back? Just look at the state I'm in. Have pity on a poor old soul!"

Feeling sorry for the old man, the gypsy told him to help himself from the pile in the wagon; and the old man kept putting them on and on and on. In the end he had on all the clothes the gypsy had bought at market.

"I'm off now, gypsy," he said at last. "I won't forget you." And without as much as a farewell he vanished into thin air.

Next morning the gypsy awoke and saw he had nothing left to take home: not a scrap of food, not a tatter of clothes. He wrung his hands in despair, but there was nothing for it: he had to go home empty-handed.

As he was traveling along the road he suddenly saw a chestnut bay astride the track. Its coat gleamed like burnished gold, its eyes flashed like rubies.

The chestnut bay would not move aside, and though the gypsy whipped on his horse it would not pull the wagon another inch, refusing to pass by the other horse. At that he lost his temper, grabbed his whip and set about the chestnut bay.

However hard he thrashed it, the horse would not move. Then, all at once, it seemed to crumble, like an ant-hill, into dust.

As he gazed dumbfounded at the heap of dust, he saw something bright glinting on the ground, and bending down, unearthed a pile of gold coins!

Of course, it was the old woodman repaying him for the food and clothes . . .

CHOOSING A BRIDE

As the gypsy wagons rolled into the foothills, the chief called a halt and they pitched their tents. About that time there were three girls of marrying age in the tribe, and their parents wished to find them husbands – honorably, the best man for each.

So they went to the chief for advice.

"Help us, *ataman* . . . this and that . . ."

The chief summoned all the young gypsy men, chose the three he thought most suitable, then told them this, "You must go into the hills and bring back whatever you deem most necessary for life."

Off they went, each to his own way.

One day passed, another and a third. As the tribe made ready for the wedding celebrations, the three men returned, upon the fourth day.

"Show us what you've brought," cried the chief.

Taking a lump of gold from his sack, the first gypsy handed it to the chieftain.

"You spent your time wisely," he said. "That's a fine gift for a bride: may you be wed to the richest of the three."

So he gained the richest bride.

"And what have you brought?" the chief asked the second lad.

Shaking his sack, the second gypsy emptied out the carcass of a deer.

119

"Your family will never die of hunger," said the chief.
"May you be wed to the plumpest of the girls."

So he gained the fattest bride.

"Well, lad, what is your gift?" inquired the chief of the
third gypsy. "Your sack seems empty; you surely have not
returned empty-handed? Did you find nothing in three whole
days?"

"I walked across the hills, *ataman*," he replied, "and saw
so much beauty. And right at the hilltop I came upon this
lovely flower . . ."

And out of his pouch he gently took a flower.

In an instant the gypsy fires faded as the blossom's light lit
up the entire valley; it eclipsed the sun's bright light, the
moon's pale rays. How the gypsies marveled at the flower's
beauty.

"Well then," the chief sighed, "since you can see beauty,
such is your fate – the prettiest bride."

And he gained the most beautiful girl in the tribe.

HOW THE DEVIL PLAYED HELL
WITH A GYPSY

A gypsy went to market and was so successful, swapping his old nag for a fine young mare, that he even had a pocketful of coins. In his joy, the gypsy popped into a tavern to celebrate, drank too much and lost his money. So the inn-keeper loaded him on to his cart and let the horse find its own way back to the encampment.

On they went, the horse pulling the cart, the tipsy gypsy riding along asleep, and behind them the new mare tied to the tail-board. Since the horse knew the road well, it had no difficulty finding the camp and the gypsy's tent.

And there it came to a halt.

In the passing of time the gypsy opened his eyes, and who should he see standing before him but the devil, clearly in bad humor.

"Where have you been, gypsy?" the devil growled.

"To market," replied the gypsy, "horse-swapping."

"Did you do well?"

"Terrific. Made a fortune."

"Where is it now? Drunk it away, no doubt!"

"What's it got to do with you?" shouted the gypsy.

"Do with me? I'll do you if I have any more cheek!"

shouted the devil, spreading his arms wide, his eyes popping out of his head.

At first the gypsy took fright; then, summoning up his courage, he snatched off his boot and lay about that devil for all he was worth. Old Nick screamed and screeched like some old dame.

"That'll teach you," he cried, beating the devil black and blue. "I'll make you whinny like an old dame."

"I'll give you old dame when I get my hands on you," cried the other. "What do you think you're up to?"

Wiping his eyes and shaking his head, the gypsy peered through the drunken mist and – heaven help us! – there stood his wife, all torn and forlorn. And not a devil to be seen.

Such things do happen, you know . . .

THE GYPSY AND THE PRIEST

Just before harvest a gypsy went to a priest in search of work.

"I'll cut you so much hay," he promised, "it'll last all winter."

"Very well," agreed the priest. "I have a large field with waist-high grass: mow it for me and earn yourself ten rubles. Fair enough?"

"Done, Your Reverence. Only it won't be a swift job. Give me some food and drink to put fire in my belly."

Well, why not? The priest gave him meat, lard, bread, a bottle of vodka – to keep the fellow going. And off to the meadow went the gypsy, his bundle of food over one shoulder, a scythe over the other.

When he came to the meadow he saw the grass was so high and thick you could stand up in it and not be seen.

First the gypsy pitched his tent, got a fire going and started to cook the food; he boiled the meat, roasted the lard in the ashes, and ate and drank to his heart's content. Then he lay down to sleep. In two days he finished off the priest's rations, yet did not do a stroke of work. When nothing remained of the food he set off back to the church house.

"Right then, Your Reverence," he said, "let's settle up."

"Have you mown the lot, gypsy?" asked the holy man.

"Every little bit," replied the gypsy. "There isn't a blade of grass left in the field; it's all cut and neatly stacked."

So the priest handed over ten rubles; yet the man lingered on.

"Toss another five in," the gypsy said. "I had a hard job with that tall grass; it was tough to cut down. If I'd known, I wouldn't have agreed to work for such a pittance."

"Oh no, gypsy boy," said the man of God, "we made a deal. Take your money and God speed."

"So you won't give me another penny?"

"No, I've settled up and have done."

"If that's the case, then let the grass grow as tall as before!"

With that the gypsy slammed the door and left.

Fearing the gypsy curse, the priest hurried off to the meadow . . . and there was the grass standing just as tall and thick as ever.

"Well I'm blessed," he gasped. "He's made the grass grow again. I shouldn't have been so stingy. Now I'll have to hire a new laborer to mow the grass!"

124

WOULD YOU LIKE TO BE RICH?

A gypsy once called on a peasant and asked: would he like to be rich?

"Who wouldn't?" exclaimed the peasant. "If only I knew how."

"I'll teach you," said the gypsy. "Follow me. Bring some gold coins with you and we'll plant them in the field. Go back tomorrow and take a look: you'll reap what you have sown."

The peasant fetched a few gold coins from his store and followed the gypsy to the fields. They planted the coins, marked the spot, and went back home. Next day they returned to take a look — and there were twice the number.

"Well, I'll be damned!" said the peasant. "Ai-yai-yai-yai-yai! I'm a rich man!"

"You don't call that rich," said the gypsy. "Come now, sow more while it's still light."

So the peasant sowed more coins; next day he hurried to the field and again found his money doubled. You should have seen him jump for joy.

"Oi-yoi-yoi-yoi-yoi! I'll soon be squire, see how many coins have grown overnight."

"To be squire you need a hundred times more. No, this won't do at all. Just go home and fetch all the gold and silver in your house. Then you can have a meal worth tasting."

Off hastened the peasant, turned his house upside down gathering all his coins, and ran back to the gypsy waiting in the field. Dig, dig, dig . . .

In the morning the peasant arrived at the field ahead of the gypsy. He could hardly wait to see the harvest: excitedly he dug and dug, but not a single coin. Just at that moment he spotted the gypsy trudging across the field, and dashed pell-mell towards him.

"Ai-yai-yai, gypsy! All my money's gone."

"What did you expect?" asked the gypsy. "We've had no rain since yesterday, see how dry the dust is. That's why all your seeds have shriveled up . . ."

As the poor peasant trooped off home, the gypsy headed for his camp, pockets jingling with gold and silver coins.

THE DEVIL AND THE GYPSY

A gypsy once took work with the devil, and one day the devil handed him a huge bucket, saying, "Go and fetch water from the well."

Off went the gypsy to the well, filled the bucket, yet could not pull it up, so heavy was it. Running back to the house, he told the devil, "Give me a spade."

"What do you want that for?"

"What's the sense in humping a pail of water every day? It'd be better to dig out the well and bring it here."

The devil was mightily surprised and not a trifle scared. "No, no, leave the well where it is," he cried. "I'll fetch water myself."

Off ran the devil to the well, pulled up the pail of water and never sent the gypsy for water again.

Shortly after this the devil needed firewood, so he sent the gypsy to gather logs for the stove. When the gypsy swung his ax in the forest he found he could not chop down a single tree, so thick were they. Running back to the house, he told the devil, "Do you have a rope that's good and strong?"

"Whatever for?"

"What's the sense of fetching firewood every day when I can tie a rope round the forest and drag the trees home?"

The devil took fright.

"No, no," he cried. "I'll fetch the wood myself."

Henceforth the devil never sent the gypsy for wood.

What was he to do with his workman? He would dearly like to see the back of him. At last he went to his chief for advice and was told, "Simple: take an iron bar and do him in!"

Now, one way or another, the gypsy learned of this chit-chat; and as night fell he put his sheepskin coat upon the shelf where he normally slept, while he snuggled into a corner beneath the shelf.

Dead on midnight, the devil crept up to the shelf with an iron bar in his hand and – CRASH! BANG! WALLOP! upon the sheepskin coat. The blows made the whole hut shake.

And from beneath the shelf came the gypsy's muffled voice, "Oh, damn! A flea just bit me."

The devil got the shock of his life and scuttled off once more to his chief.

"What am I to do?" he wailed. "I walloped him with my iron bar and he thought it was a flea bite."

"If you cannot kill him, you'd better pay him off," the elder said.

So the devil gave the gypsy a full purse of gold and sent him packing.

God alone knows how much time went by, but eventually the devil began to bemoan the loss of his gold; and he set out in pursuit of the gypsy. On finding his old workman, the devil cried, "I want to settle accounts with you, gypsy. I bet I can toss this iron bar higher than you can. If I win you give back my gold; if you win I'll double the sum."

It was agreed.

When the devil tossed his iron bar it took an hour for it to land. And as the gypsy went to pick it up he found it was too heavy for him to lift. Looking up at the sky, he shouted out, "Hey, devil! See my brother the crane flying through the sky? I'll toss him your iron bar and he'll be glad of it to shoe God's horses with."

Grabbing the gypsy's sleeve, the devil cried, "No, no, I don't want to lose my iron bar. You win, but let's try something else. Whoever runs faster will take the gold, double or quits."

"First you pit yourself against my son," the gypsy said. "See, there he is over there; he's only three days old."

It was agreed.

So the gypsy ran off, caught a hare and showed it to the devil. "Now off you go!"

As the gypsy released the hare, the devil rushed off in pursuit; but the hare hopped and skipped through fields and bog, leaving the poor devil far behind.

When the devil, tired and bedraggled, returned to the gypsy, he panted, "One more try: whoever beats the other at wrestling takes all the gold. Agreed?"

"You're too tired to beat me," said the gypsy. "You'd better take on my old grandfather first."

Thereupon the gypsy led the devil to a bear's den in a cave, and pushed him in. The angry bear was not happy at being woken up so rudely and grabbed the intruder in his strong arms; he all but skinned the poor devil alive before chucking him out on his ear.

But the devil would not give in. "Just one last test," he begged the gypsy. "Whoever can stamp the harder wins the contest, fair enough?"

"As you wish," agreed the gypsy.

When the devil stamped his foot upon a rock it crumbled to dust; in the meantime the gypsy had filled his boot with water. So when he stamped his foot upon a rock, water oozed out of the boot and the rock was dripping wet.

The devil could not believe his eyes. "You've won again, gypsy!" he cried in despair. "Now this is positively the final test: whoever whistles louder will take the gold, and have done with it."

129

When the devil whistled the piercing sound went round the whole wide world. But the gypsy, who had stuffed his ears with moss, just laughed.

"Now when I whistle you'll go deaf and blind and dumb. So you'd better shut tight your eyes and ears right now."

Shutting his eyes tight and blocking up his ears, the devil stood waiting . . . as the gypsy swung his cudgel and brought it crashing down on the devil's head: once, twice, three times.

After the third blow the devil cried, "Stop, stop, no more whistling or my head will burst! You win, here, take all my gold and leave me in peace."

With a chuckle, the gypsy swung the sack of gold across his back and went on his way; as for the devil, he hurried home and never bothered the gypsy again.

THE TYRANT CZAR

There was once a cruel Czar who would cut off heads for the slightest fault, even for his amusement. And this tyrant would spare no one. Those to suffer most were gypsies camped not far distant from the city.

One time a sentry seized a young gypsy, whether for stealing horses or for the fun of it I do not know.

The Czar's verdict: off with his head! But not simply that: all gypsies from far and near were to be present at the execution.

So the gypsies were rounded up and brought to see a gypsy head roll. As the Czar gave the sign to begin, the executioner raised his ax and . . . just at that moment there came a shout:

STOP!

Out of the crowd rushed a pretty gypsy girl, throwing herself at the tyrant's feet.

"May the heavens bless you, Czar," she cried. "Cut off my head, but spare this man."

On his dais, the Czar rubbed his chin, then smiled, "Very well, I'll spare him. But you'll have to dance for me, and if it doesn't please me I'll behead you both."

A fiddler began to play, the girl's shoulders began to shake, her arms twisted and turned, her feet moved briskly to the lively tune. And all about her the gypsies clapped their hands and stamped their feet in time to the tune.

When the dance came to an end, the crowd about the square buzzed with excitement, entranced by the gypsy dance.

Yet the cruel Czar was not moved. With an evil chuckle, he shouted out, "Have them both beheaded!"

It was done.

Yet the moment their heads fell, a terrible whirlwind blew up, thunder boomed and lightning flashed. With a deafening crash, the royal stand collapsed, burying and crushing the tyrant Czar beneath the bodies of those above. Thus was justice done.

Beware all tyrants who would oppress gypsies – the gypsy curse will strike you down!

ZAPYLA THE GYPSY

There was once a wealthy gypsy, on good terms even with dukes and merchants. And that gypsy had an only son whose name was Zapyla, as handsome as he was strong. Not only that, he had a head on his shoulders too, a real Rom without a doubt.

Meanwhile, within another clan there lived a gypsy family with an only daughter whose name was Rosa. And Rosa had been brought up in strict seclusion. No one saw her face — though she was fabled to be very beautiful — and she was not permitted to look on other men.

But you cannot hide from gossip, and the young pair, Zapyla and Rosa, came to hear of one another from what folk said. In the passing of the days Zapyla had a dream in which an old man came to him. "Go to such-and-such a place, my lad," he said. "There you'll find fair Rosa, daughter of wealthy gypsies."

Next morning Zapyla told his father of his plan to pay the lovely girl a visit.

"No, no, my son," said his father, wringing his hands. "Sons of princes have sought her hand, but none has even as much as seen her shadow."

But the lad would not listen. He took the finest steed from the stables, saddled it and rode off on his quest.

Whether he was long on his way I cannot say, but in the

passing of time he came upon a cowherd tending cattle on the estate where Rosa lived. And the cowherd was dressed so shabbily it was painful just to look at him: all tatters and tears and patches.

"Take off those rags," called Zapyla, "and don my clothes; I'll wear yours."

"Come now, Sire," said the cowherd, taking the smart young man for some rich baron, "don't mock a poor cowherd."

"I do not joke; do as I say."

So the cowherd gladly took off his tatters and gave them to Zapyla, who did likewise. Then Zapyla told the man, "Here's my horse, keep it safe till I return. As for my clothes, wear them yourself, tend the cattle in them, I don't care."

And off he went on foot, coming at last to the camp where Rosa lived. At once he approached Rosa's father to bid him good-day.

"Where are you from? What tribe are you?" asked the man suspiciously.

"Wait a moment," said Zapyla, shaking his head. "A God-fearing man would first give me food and drink, then ask about my kin."

So he was fed and given drink, then asked more questions.

He told them this and that, and asked if there was work with horses. Rosa's father was still suspicious, and first consulted his wife.

"See here, there's a gypsy asking for work, a shabby fellow. What if he's a vagabond or thief?"

The fair Rosa heard her father's word and called from inside the tent, "What are you afraid of, Father? You always think ill of people. He says he's hungry, cold and tired. Surely we can find him clothing? Surely we can spare a crust of bread?"

In short, Rosa's father took on the gypsy lad. And since he

134

had a fair number of horses – some say a score or more, others even a hundred – he gave Zapyla the job of looking after them. The lad knew his job all right, kept the herd all fit and smart, much to the liking of the master.

"That's a real Rom," he would tell his wife.

One time Rosa's father made ready for the local horse fair and before leaving he told Zapyla, "I'm going to a fair, dealing in horses the gypsy way. Bring me such-and-such horses at once."

Zapyla caught the horses for the master, then asked a favor, "Why not let me go with you? Give me the worst horse you have and see how I do at the fair."

The master roared with laughter. "I suppose you could learn a trick or two from me. Only you won't sell much with your knees and backside poking through your breeches!"

"I'll go in what I stand, master. Folk must accept me for what I am."

"Very well," said the old man, shrugging his shoulders. "Please yourself."

So they came to the fair. Well-to-do gypsies paid their respects to Rosa's father, but all ignored Zapyla. The fair buzzed with business all day long: folk traded, swapped and haggled, cheated one another as best they could. In short, the old man sold all his horses and stood waiting for his groom. But he soon got the shock of his life, for down the road came Zapyla leading three fine racehorses on the bridle.

"This is what I earned for your old nag," he said, taking a pile of coins from his pocket, and showing off the steeds.

The old man's eyes misted over, his hair bristled, and he whistled through his teeth. "You're no fool, that's for sure."

And off they went laughing together to the nearest tavern.

Months passed, but still Zapyla had gained no glimpse of the beautiful Rosa. Even though he had won her father's confidence he was kept well away from the master's tent. One day, however, the old man had to depart for a few days with his wife. That gave Zapyla an idea.

Rounding up the horses, he drove them straight towards the tents, shouting, "Rosa, Rosa, save yourself, the horses are loose and will trample down your tent!"

There was nothing for it: she had to run outside. The instant Zapyla saw her his eyes clouded over, his hair stood on end, his heart caught fire. And despite his ragamuffin looks, Rosa could see he was a bold and handsome fellow. As she looked at him her face burnt with a scarlet flame.

Recovering her senses, Rosa cried, "Where are you driving the herd? Round them up at once."

"Why don't you?" he shouted back. "Take your father's whip and round them up yourself."

Her temper rising, she snatched up the whip, shouting, "Right, out of my way!"

And she set about the cheeky groom with her father's whip, giving him a good thrashing.

"Hit away!" he cried. "It's no more than I deserve: I've gazed my fill and have to pay."

His words only enflamed her more, and she lashed him even harder, until her strength gave out.

"Well?" he said. "Are you done now?"

Her cheeks flushed with anger mixed with shame, she put down her whip and looked closer at the young man before her, blood coursing down his face.

It touched her heart. Taking a tub into the tent, she heated water, sat him in the tub and washed him clean – just like a good wife washes a husband.

When that was done, she offered him her hand to settle the quarrel. "Let's be friends," she said. "Come, stay with me until my parents return."

She had fallen in love with Zapyla, and he with her. So they lived together as man and wife within the family tent. When her father came home, he looked and stared: the horses were running wild, the tent flap was open, and there soon appeared Rosa arm in arm with the groom.

"What are you about, daughter?" he cried in a fury. "Are you mad?"

Rosa told her father what had happened, keeping nothing back. And the old man could do nothing about it now; the knot was well and truly tied, no man could untie it.

Some time later, Zapyla said to Rosa's father, "I wish to prove my worth. The duke has a wild horse whom no one can ride – neither gypsies, nor *gadjes*, neither rich, nor poor. I'll fetch that horse for you."

"You're a rascal," sighed the old man. "One misfortune on top of another: you can't go stealing from the duke. If he catches you, he'll kill you and all the gypsies will suffer."

"I won't steal it," said Zapyla. "I intend to swap it for your old nag with the crooked snout."

"You're more stupid than I thought," the old man snorted. "Don't you know the duke's horse is priceless? Many wish to buy it but no man is rich enough to pay the price."

All the same, Zapyla saddled the old bag of bones and trotted off towards the duke's mansion. Coming to a field, he jumped down and wrote on the nag's front hoof:

> *Prancer and dancer*
> *Costs a dozen heads*

Then off he trotted until he reached the cowherd with whom he had swapped his clothes.

Once more they exchanged their clothes and Zapyla continued on his way to the duke. When he arrived he told the guards, "Inform your master that such-and-such a notable has arrived."

The duke was duly told and came out in person to meet the elegant gypsy.

"I have an uncommon horse," he told the duke. "It has no rival in the whole wide world; it may not look much to the untrained eye, but it has astounding gifts. Just see what is inscribed upon its hoof."

Bending down in curiosity, the duke read,

> *Prancer and dancer*
> *Costs a dozen heads*

The duke was startled. "How can I own such a magic horse?" he wondered.

"A fine steed, yes indeed, most unusual," he said. "Tell me what you want for it."

"I have heard you have a wild steed," Zapyla said. "I might swap it for mine."

Eager to own this unusual beast, the duke ordered his groom to fetch the horse at once and give it to the gypsy. That done, Zapyla took the duke's wild steed, saddled it and rode off on his way.

Meanwhile, Rosa's father was watching for his son-in-law's return when he spotted the duke's famous steed ridden by Zapyla dressed in smart attire.

"Heaven help us!" he cried. "That Zapyla'll be the death of all of us. He must have stolen that steed and the duke's best clothes as well. We'll all be hanged for this!"

When the horse and rider drew up, the old man cried, "How can this be?"

"Well, Sir," said Zapyla, "you had an old bag of bones, worth no more than three rubles to you. But with a good master, the horse is priceless. Since I have proved myself a good master of your horse, I shall be an even better master of your daughter."

A wedding feast was held to which all the gypsies of the world were invited. And the happy pair lived in good health and cheer for many a long and prosperous year.

THE SORCERER AND HIS APPRENTICE

There was once an old sorcerer who lived with his young wife. And a wandering gypsy came roaming in those parts seeking work. He had long sought his fortune, yet so far had found none at all. He had not a penny in his pocket, nor even a horse. All he had were his quick wits.

The sorcerer was glad to take on the wayfarer as his apprentice: he could help him prepare his spells, groom the horses, and assist about the house.

One day passed, and another, and the gypsy began to notice the sorcerer's wife eyeing him as he went about his chores. He did not mind since she was indeed a pretty soul. And all would have gone well had the sorcerer not found out. Sorcerers are sorcerers; you cannot keep secrets from them. And he was not overjoyed to see his wife flirting with the gypsy.

So – *whisht!* – he turned her into a gray mare and banished her to the stables. It was the gypsy's job to groom her.

"Now you can flirt with her all you wish!" chuckled the sorcerer.

In the stables the gypsy wept, for he had dearly loved the pretty maid. And suddenly he heard a human voice. "Grieve not, my love, everything will turn out fair."

The gypsy's eyes grew wide with surprise as he saw it was the mare talking. From then on he kept the mare so clean and tidy, tended her so lovingly that it was ever a pleasure to see her.

That did not please the sorcerer at all. So he decided to do away with the meddlesome gypsy.

"Listen, gypsy," he said one day. "Go down to the sea, sail to an island, light a fire and wait there: at midnight the waves will part and a carriage and pair will emerge. Go to that carriage, open the door and glance inside: I left my ring there. If you fetch it here, I'll take the spell from my wife and let you marry her."

With head bowed low, the gypsy returned to the stables.

"What grieves you, my beloved?" asked the mare.

"This and that." The story was told; the gypsy was in tears.

"Go to the sea," she said at last. "All will be well. Just coat yourself with tar so that the steeds cannot bite you; then fetch the ring and come home straightaway."

The gypsy did all she told him and returned with the ring.

The sorcerer pretended to be pleased.

"Well done, gypsy!" he cried. "I'll keep my word and remove the spell. But just look at you, covered in tar; no decent woman will look at you like that. I'll heat up some milk for you to bathe in."

Sensing some trickery, the gypsy went sadly to the stables to tell the mare the story.

"Don't you fret, my darling," said the mare. "Do exactly as I tell you. The sorcerer will heat some milk in a cauldron and make you bathe in boiling milk. But fear not: the moment you hear me neigh, jump straight into the boiling milk."

All went as foretold: the sorcerer boiled milk and told the gypsy to jump into the cauldron. So the lad boldly undressed and stood waiting for the mare to neigh.

"What's the delay?" shouted the sorcerer. "Are you scared?"

"I'm scared of nothing," the gypsy replied. "By gypsy

custom we say a few secret words before we take a bath."

"Go on then, say your secret words," said the sorcerer with a smirk, pushing more wood beneath the pot.

Raising his hands to the sky, the gypsy muttered, "May the sun burn you to a cinder, cruel sorcerer!"

Just at that moment the mare gave a neigh and he leapt forthwith into the boiling milk . . . And when he emerged he was the handsomest man in all the world.

Envy burned inside the sorcerer. How had that happened? How could a humble gypsy become so fair? Surely a mighty sorcerer could become even handsomer!

Without more ado, he took off his clothes and jumped into the pot of boiling milk . . . and was burnt to a cinder.

At once the spell unfolded from the mare and she was again a young and lovely maid. And from then on she and the gypsy lived together to their hearts' content.

WHY GYPSIES ARE SCATTERED ABOUT THE EARTH

This happened long ago.

A gypsy and his family were traveling along. His horse was skinny and none too steady on his legs, and as the gypsy's family grew he found it harder to pull the weighty wagon. Soon the wagon was so full of children tumbling over one another, the poor horse could barely stumble along the rutted track.

As the wagon rumbled on, veering first to the left, then rocking to the right, pots and pans would go tumbling out, and now and then a barefoot child pitched headlong upon the ground.

It was not so bad in daylight, then you could pick up your pots and tiny tots; but you could not see them in the dark. In any case, who could keep count of such a tribe? And the nag plodded on its way.

The gypsy traveled right round the earth; and everywhere he went he left a child behind: more and more and more.

And that, you see, is how gypsies came to be scattered about the earth!

GLOSSARY

ataman	chieftain
Baro Shero	chief (lit. "big head")
beng	devil
Calo Rom	Black Gypsy
chiavala	lad
chiavalei	lads
Devaley	God
drom	road
Dza devlesa	God go with you
gadje	non-gypsy
kesali	forest spirit
kumpanias	clans, tribes
mora	friend
much	friend
nivasi	water spirit
Rom	Gypsy
Romaly	Gypsies
shoshka	tent pole (Russían)
vaida	Gypsy chief

DZA DEVLESA!